Happiness
DOESN'T JUST
HAPPEN

WADE BURLESON

Happiness
DOESN'T JUST
HAPPEN

LEARNING TO BE
CONTENT
REGARDLESS OF YOUR
CIRCUMSTANCES

York Street Press

Enid, Oklahoma 73703 USA

Happiness Doesn't Just Happen©2003 by Wade Burleson

Library of Congress Control Number: 2003113983
ISBN: 0-9745502-0-5

Cover design by Kris Vculek
Production coordinated by Mona Loewen

To the gracious people
of Emmanuel, Enid

Acknowledgments

For more than a decade, the gracious people of Emmanuel Baptist Church, Enid, Oklahoma, have showered my family and me with their love. This book would not have been possible were it not for their encouragement and support.

Every week Barbara Ebert, my executive secretary, types a manuscript of at least two sermons I have preached. The seeds for this book were planted at the keyboard of her computer as she listened to countless hours of audio. Her work is invaluable.

Mona Loewen is the professional who made this book possible. I am grateful for her contributions from beginning to end. It is difficult for me to imagine producing a book without her expertise.

I meet with a group of men every Tuesday morning for an hour of discipleship. These carpenters, businessmen, accountants, air force pilots, attorneys, civic leaders, and self-employed professionals are extraordinarily astute theologically. I often have said that I have never been around a group of men, even seminarians, who have such an understanding of God's grace. A great number of illustrations in this book come from my free-flow discussions with these men every Tuesday morning.

Finally, I want to thank my wife, Rachelle, for living out in her life the principles of grace that I know to be true in my head. She has taught me by her actions more than I could ever express with my words.

Wade Burleson
November 2003

Contents

A self-made man has no one to blame but himself.
Anonymous

*God's grace turns pebbles into pearls, sickness into health,
weakness into strength and wants into abundance.*
Thomas Brooks

Introduction

Happiness Doesn't Just Happen is a book for those of us
who sometimes find life taking a turn for the worse, just
when we expected it to cruise down the highway toward
happiness.

It is also a book for others of us who are happy in life
because our situations are wonderful. It serves as a written
caution not to base our happiness on wonderful careers,
money in the bank, stellar reputations, or any other positive
event in life. Our circumstances will eventually change. If our
happiness has been dependent on those good things, which
we will one day lose, we might find ourselves in despair or
even depression.

I want to help you discover how happiness can be experienced *independent* of your circumstances. This might sound
impossible at first, but I think you will find it is not as un-
thinkable as it seems. There is nothing you must *do*, but there
is something you must *learn*.

Happiness Doesn't Just Happen is not a self-help book. Self-help will always *eventually* lead to self-failure. This is a discovery book about God's sovereign grace. God speaks clearly and authoritatively regarding our happiness and enjoyment in life. He tells us that *true contentment or happiness comes to those who have learned to rest in His grace.*

If we are seeking happiness in our circumstances, or in anything other than God's grace, we are destined to eventually lose any personal satisfaction we have found. But if we learn to revel in the truths of God's eternal grace, then, no matter the shifting state of our circumstances, we can experience real joy.

HAPPINESS WILL COME

I am basing the following chapters on the promises of God. If you don't believe God's word, then you won't be able to accept the conclusions of this book. But if you trust the veracity of Scripture, there is the very real possibility that you are a few reading hours away from finding a freedom you have never fathomed. *"You shall know the truth and the truth shall set you free"* (John 8:32).

I will take you to the verse where Paul uses this exact phrase, *"I have unlocked the mystery of contentment,"* and I'll show you that it is possible for a Christian to be *happy in every circumstance of life.*

The happiness that will come is not that slapstick silly happiness that you see painted on the faces of televangelists, but a genuine contentment and joy that comes from within and is independent of your circumstances.

I will give you the key for unlocking the mystery of happiness in Chapter Two. In the remaining chapters I will help you work that key into the lock of your life.

Some of the "I am——" statements in Chapters Three through Fifteen will mean more to you than others. However, all of the "I am——" statements are true of you whether they strike an emotional chord now or not.

Life has a way of hitting different notes, at different times, along the keyboard of experience. For this reason *Happiness Doesn't Just Happen* can be read, and then reread, depending on one's station in life.

Use this book as an athlete would a playbook. Go to it on a regular basis when you start feeling blue because of your circumstances. God's grace is good news regardless of application, but my prayer is that His grace may become so explosively beautiful to *you* that your outlook on life is drastically changed for the better.

SPIRIT WORK

The Apostle Paul thanked God for what He had done in the lives of the people of Thessalonica through *"belief of the truth and the work of the Spirit"* (II Thessalonians 2:13). Ordinary people in Thessalonica had been given an extraordinary gift. They had been taught by the Spirit of God to appreciate what God had done for them. As a result, their hearts were filled with *"everlasting comfort and good hope through grace"* (II Thessalonians 2:14).

I would ask that you pause before you begin reading Chapter One and ask the Lord to graciously help you see the truth of His word. Let Him know that you expect to have questions, and even be hurt, by what you come to know about your condition apart from His grace.

But ask God not to leave you in despair. He is the *blessed Hope*. Request that He reveal to you, through His word, the great power of His sovereign grace.

For you see, true happiness is solely dependent upon His grace.

*All men are endowed by their Creator
with certain unalienable rights;
that among these are life, liberty,
and the pursuit of happiness.*

The Declaration of Independence

Chapter 1
UNHAPPINESS HAPPENS

When calamity comes, the wicked are brought down,
but even in death the righteous have a refuge.
Proverbs 14:32

If I were an inventor and could make a pill that would have the power to make you happy, I imagine I could become a very rich man. Not only would you buy the pill from me, but you would tell your friends and they would say, "I want that pill."

I am not a pill pitchman. But I believe if you read the rest of this book carefully, you will come to understand that happiness *is* a possibility for every believer. I believe you will come to the conclusion that you can be happy regardless of your circumstances. If you see what the word of God says, you can unlock the secret of being happy in whatever state you are in.

But it does not *just happen.* The Declaration of Independence says we have the right to *pursue* happiness. It would not say the "*pursuit* of happiness" if happiness were something easily attained.

We are often deluded in our efforts to find happiness. We deny our sinfulness, base our goodness on our performance, and have not even begun to understand God's grace. As a result, our happiness changes to unhappiness as often as our circumstances change from good to bad.

DISCONTENTMENT WITH CIRCUMSTANCES

I wish you could listen in to what I hear from countless people through counseling (I am sure that other pastors would verify this in their own ministries). I am inundated with people who say, "Pastor, I am so unhappy, I really need help."

I have never had anyone come to me and say, "Pastor, would you visit with me for a while? I'm extremely happy, and I don't know what to do."

When I ask unhappy people what is troubling them, they might say that it is their spouse, or their job, or a particular struggle that they are dealing with. The source of their unhappiness usually comes down to discontentment with their circumstances.

Some of you who have recently experienced tragedy might say to me, "Pastor, you haven't gone through the loss of a spouse. You haven't gone through the death of a child. You haven't gone through heartache like I have. You do not know pain like I do." I do not make light of your hurt or pain. I recognize there are dark, painful days for all of us. I also recognize that sometimes there are physical causes for our unhappiness. Hormonal changes, chemical imbalances and disease can contribute to feelings of depression.

That's my point—unhappiness happens.

THE NATURE OF UNHAPPINESS

Unhappiness is a *natural* occurrence for every human being. In describing human happiness, my father has said, "Happiness happens when 'happenstances' happen to be happy."[1] What he means is: if circumstances are good, a person is happy; if circumstances are pleasing, he or she is fulfilled.

When the family is in good shape, when the job provides great income, when everything is the way one thinks it ought to be, happiness happens. We can find some people who are extremely happy because they have everything they could ever imagine that could bring happiness to their lives—a beautiful wife, a successful husband, beautiful children, a great job.

> ❧
>
> *Happiness happens when "happenstances" happen to be happy.*
>
> ❧

But mark my words—when things turn south, when things go bad, happiness goes down the drain because for most people happiness is dependent upon "happenstances" or circumstances. *Happiness* during difficult circumstances is the exception, not the norm.

A Believer's Unhappiness

Believers in Jesus Christ, like everyone else, can struggle with happiness coming and going in relation to circumstances. Christians often do not have a feeling of inward happiness or joy because their circumstances are miserable.

However, the believer has the ability to *learn* how to be content, joyful, and happy *independent of circumstances.* This learning is due to a growing comprehension of God's grace.

When things go bad for us and our happiness vanishes, it is because it is dependent upon other circumstances, people, or events. We are what psychologists call "co-dependent." Christians may not like that word, but it does describe us who *depend* upon others for happiness. We have not learned to be content regardless of our circumstances.

Blame for our unhappiness usually starts closest to home with husband, wife, father, mother, child, or grandchild. Then it moves out to boss, employee, schoolmates, boyfriend, girlfriend, or any person or situation beyond our control. We peg this person or that problem as the cause of our unhappiness.

So we try to change the people around us or change our circumstances in pursuit of happiness. If we see our spouse as the root of our unhappiness, we become controlling and manipulative. If we find ourselves in a situation we cannot control, then we flee. We might change jobs because we cannot handle it anymore. A pastor might leave a church because he just cannot handle his unhappiness, which he blames on the deacons or the people in the congregation.

FALSE HAPPINESS

Some try to pursue happiness by finding substitutes for genuine contentment, which only leads to false happiness.

They turn to possessions, hobbies, drugs, sex, work, or alcohol. They become alcoholics, addicts, or compulsive people. They take it all in, and for a time it pumps them up. But their addictions simply mask the pain in their hearts. False happiness is false because it is not rooted within the soul.

Some of you reading this are thinking, "This does not apply to me. I am basically happy. I am not struggling with contentment." You are thinking, "Yes, this book is a good study" and, "Yes, I will read it; but for the purpose of using it to teach and help others."

However, very few of us, if any, can avoid the struggle in learning how to be content. No one has arrived.

The measure of our unhappiness can often be discovered by discerning the level of internal discontentment in our lives. Before we continue, I challenge you to look inside yourself and see if you have the following signs of discontentment.

FIVE MARKS OF DISCONTENTMENT

There are five marks of discontentment that are signs pointing to a soul dependent upon circumstances for happiness.

Envy is a sure mark of discontentment. Our soul is locked in unhappiness when envy reigns, or rules, and takes the throne of our hearts. Dr. John Gill says, "Where the sin of envy is predominant, a man can have no true contentment of mind." *"Envy is the rottenness of the bones"* (Proverbs 14:30b).

> *Where the sin of envy is predominant, a man can have no true contentment of mind.*

Max Lucado writes that envy is a "fire in the heart, which, left unchecked, can burst into a hungry flame and consume all that is consumable." It can lead to loneliness, sickness, and violence.[2] *"Wrath kills the foolish man, and envy slays the silly one"* (Job 5:2).

I have a personal understanding of envy in the life of a pastor. We pastors can become the most discontented individuals on the face of the earth. Every time I go to my denomination's convention, either my discontentment or the discontentment of my peers can be seen within five minutes. We talk about who is at what church, how someone else's church is doing, how other churches are growing. We look around and see another pastor promoted to a larger church or another brother given a prestigious position, and then envy comes. "How can my name be as well known as his? Why can't I be at a church as large as his?"

If I cannot be excited about my peers advancing to large churches, to places of prestige, to television ministries, and other areas of leadership; then I am envious. *When I am envious, it is a sure sign of a lack of understanding of who I am in Christ.*

What about you? What if promotion time comes and, for some reason, the boss chooses a co-worker to be promoted over you? Does it really get into your craw that you are bypassed? I am not saying that you should not desire or pursue the promotion, but if you cannot be happy for the success and promotion of the other person, then you are plagued with discontentment and envy.

You might say, "But you are not human if it doesn't hurt when you're bypassed and someone else is promoted." You are speaking more truth than you realize. Human nature apart from Christ will always be envious.

If we begin to understand God's grace to us, then we can say it is all right if we are not promoted in this earthly life because we have been given the greatest promotion of all. We, as believers, reign with our Lord. We are priests and kings (Revelation 5:10). We are "co-heirs" with Jesus Christ (Romans 8:17). We already reign with the true King of kings and Lord of lords.

Covetousness is another sure symptom of discontentment. Covetousness is an unwarranted, ungodly, and immoderate desire to have more possessions. *"Let your conversation be without covetousness; and be content with such things as you have"* (Hebrews 13:5).

How do we know if there is covetousness in our lives? I can break it down into three words. *Credit card debt.* Notice, I said *"credit card"* debt—not just any kind of debt. Sometimes we need to borrow for home mortgages or to start businesses. Scripture does not say that all debt is wrong. However, credit card debt is debt for possessions that do not last. These possessions soon fade and lose their luster.

Credit card debt is a sign that we do not understand who we are by the grace of God. We think we *need* (but we actually just *want*) certain things in order to make us happy. We *want* (not *need*) better clothes. We *want* to eat out at the finest restaurants. We *want* to have the best television possible. We believe we *need* to have *things* to make our lives exciting. Because we cannot wait until we can afford it (we want instant gratification), we put it on the credit card.

> *Credit card debt is a sign that we do not understand who we are by the grace of God.*

All of us at times desire, and need, to have certain things: a larger automobile or home when the family is growing, better tools or equipment to make a living, appropriate clothing for work and activities, and so forth. Having material possessions is not wrong. What is wrong and sinful is the unwarranted, ungodly, and immoderate desire to get what we can. My father describes the desires of a discontent person as wanting to "get what you can, can what you get, and then sit on the can."

One of the best ways to tell if we are covetous is if we are willing to freely *give* all that we have for the good of others. If the Lord has been gracious financially, praise Him for it.

Be on guard if you find yourself unwilling to give any away. Be sensitive to the needs of others and be generous. The greatest people to be around are givers who give freely because it is what they enjoy doing.

A third mark of personal unhappiness is prideful ambition. This is a desire to bow to none but to be above all. After Alexander the Great thought he had conquered the whole world, he sat down and wept because there was not another world to conquer.

Sometimes it is difficult to distinguish prideful ambition from a healthy desire to do our best. As Christians, everything we do should be done for the glory of God.

Prideful ambition, however, is a sin. It is destructive. It is when we promote ourselves, submitting to no one, being the servant to none; but, rather, wanting everyone to be our servant.

This is played out in the home when we have to win every argument, when we have to be the ruler of the roost. It all has to go our way, and we cannot allow someone to say to us, "You're wrong."

Prideful ambition is the kind of thinking that says: "I don't care what Jesus Christ says about this area of my life. I am feeling unhappy so I am going to do whatever I can to make myself happy."

Unfortunately, our church has had some members who decided they would be happier with someone other than their own spouse. Our church is very loving and does not condemn these people who are living in immorality. We go to them and tell them what God says, that they are to remain faithful to their spouse and not break up their family and leave their children. We tell them we love them and do not condemn them for their temptation, or even for following through with it. But we try to lead them to repentance and back to their spouse and family. Sadly, many of them tell me, "Pastor, I don't expect you to understand what I'm doing; but I have prayed about this, and I have a peace that this is what will make my life happy."

God will never give peace for a direct violation of His word. So the peace they are feeling is a false peace and a false happiness. I explain to them if God does not lead them to repentance, even though our church will continue to love them and not condemn them, then we will no longer treat them as those who have experienced God's grace (i.e. "Christians"). As you would expect, this usually makes them furious with me. They tell me to go away and please leave them alone. Many times, months later, we will hear that they are no longer with the one they left their family for and their life is miserable. Independence from God always brings misery in life.

If we will not listen to what Christ says, if we say "No!" to Him and insist on doing our own thing, then prideful ambition is present. And, no matter how we try to hide it, *we are discontent and unhappy.*

The fourth sign of a lack of soul satisfaction is complaining, which can be defined as murmuring about one's circumstances, troubles, or afflictions. The apostle Paul says, *"In everything give thanks"* (I Thessalonians 5:18a). We are told, *"Neither murmur ye"* (I Corinthians 10:10a KJV), and *"Wherefore does a living man complain?"* (Lamentations 3:39a). If a person is constantly complaining about circumstances, then discontentment is boiling under the surface.

At work and at home, how often do we find ourselves complaining about another individual? How often do we find ourselves saying or thinking, "You know, if so and so would just simply do this," or "If my husband were only better at this," or "If my wife would only have dinner on the table at the time I prefer."

I grew up in a very godly Christian home, but we showed little affection or emotion toward one another. No one is really at fault in that. God, in His providence, allowed me to grow up in that home. Doctrine was very important, and I thank God that I learned doctrine. However, my family just did not know how to express love for each other on an emotional level. As a result, we began to conceive love as others doing things the way we wanted them done. If they did things the way we wanted, we would say, "Well, it's evident you love me." We put expectations on each other. We put strings on each other. We controlled and manipulated each other.

Over the years, my mom and dad have learned to rest in the grace of God. They have begun to relate to their children in totally different ways. For instance, my mom recently said to me, "Wade, I want you to be a son that loves to come by my home and loves to just sit down and talk with me; to pick up the phone and say, 'Mom, how are you doing?'" (Now that is something I have never done. I have not even known how to do that, but it does not mean I do not love my mom.)

Then my mom stopped. She said, "You know what? I'm doing to you what I've done all your life. I am placing expectations on you." She said, "I must stop. Wade, I want you to know you don't have to call me. You don't have to come by. You don't have to do any of that stuff. Just be yourself. I love you the way you are." My mom understands grace.

If you have grown up where people complain about what you do, or complain because you do not do this or that, then your understanding and concept of love will be the same way. You will complain about others. When you complain, it signifies a lack of understanding of who you and others are in Christ.

Complaining time after time after time about other people, our circumstances, our troubles, or our afflictions is the opposite of contentment. Complaining indicates that we are dependent upon these things in order to be happy. Why not, like the apostle Paul, come to the place where we can say we are happy regardless of whether or not circumstances or others around us change?

The final sign of our unhappiness—sinful anger—is a big one. The extent of our anger is a key indicator of whether or not there is contentment in our lives. A lot of anger equals very little contentment.

Not all anger is sin—even Jesus showed righteous anger. *Sinful* anger is characterized by resentment and bitterness. Those who let the sun go down on their anger and become bitter with others are full of discontentment. They harbor a grudge toward those who have wronged them. They are resentful and desire to take revenge.

Others just explode in anger. This type of sinful anger is an emotional response of rage directed toward those who do not meet one's expectations. People with this type of anger can be extremely abusive to those around them. Their spouses and their children are often injured physically and emotionally by their angry outbursts.

Anger is not always outward and explosive. Anger can turn within. When it turns within, it can destroy us over time. We can be so tied up in knots that we sleep fitfully. We get spasms in our backs

> *The worst of slaves is he whom anger rules*

and ulcers in our stomachs. We brood, suffer depression, become quiet and withdrawn.

Sometimes we are so full of anger, and we don't even know why. Recently a young lady shared with me that she is angry with her kids and her skin crawls with bitterness when her husband walks into the room, and she does not know why she is so full of anger.

Philip Brooks says, "The worst of slaves is he whom anger rules." Paul writes, *"Let all bitterness, wrath, anger, clamor, and evil speaking, be put away from you, with all malice"* (Ephesians 4:31).

ARE YOU UNHAPPY?

If you recognize any of these five marks of discontentment within yourself, then unhappiness is happening. But there is hope! This is the first step in the process of learning to be happy.

Until we realize that no person and no problem is the cause of our unhappiness, and until we realize that a deficient understanding of the grace of God in our lives is the reason that we lack self-sufficiency, joy, and contentment, we will never make progress in overcoming our misery.

Some of you might be thinking, "Wait a minute! I don't know anything about God's grace, and I have not even begun to find out what the Bible says about grace, but I'm *not unhappy*. In fact, I am *very happy!*"

Maybe you are happy now—but just wait.

There will come a day when your circumstances *will* change. Misery awaits you right around the corner. And if your happiness and contentment are dependent upon your circumstances, then when your good circumstances turn bad, your happiness will be gone like a swift ship.

You and I can only rightly evaluate whether we are content and happy in our souls, regardless of our circumstances, if our circumstances are terrible.

If your circumstances are terrible, but you are content and happy, then you do not need to continue to read this book. You have already unlocked the mystery. But if your circumstances are terrible and you lack genuine happiness, contentment, and joy—then read on. Soul satisfaction awaits you.

If your theology is self-oriented, rather than God-oriented, you will always be struggling for happiness and contentment.

You cannot be content until you learn what God is doing, by His grace, in your soul and life.

Chapter 2
THE KEY TO HAPPINESS

For I have learned, in whatsoever state I am,
therewith to be content.
Philippians 4:11b KJV

I hope you are not a person who believes there is something wrong in desiring to be happy. Some Christians teach a kind of stoicism that elevates suffering and misery. A few will even criticize a pastor if he tells a joke from the pulpit.

According to Phil Yancy:

> Nowadays in the church sober-mindedness has won the day. Evangelicals are responsible citizens whom most people appreciate as neighbors but don't want to spend much time with. Theologians with long faces lecture on "the imperatives of the faith." Television evangelists with every hair in place (often dyed) confidently name the Antichrist, predict the end of the world, and announce how to have a prosperous and healthy life in the meanwhile. The religious right calls for moral regeneration, and ordinary Christians point to temperance, industriousness, and achievement as primary proofs of their faith.[1]

Some of these pulpit-pounding expositors have ignored the wisdom of the past. A few hundred years ago, the Presbyterians got together and wrote the Westminster Confession of Faith. The Shorter Catechism of that Westminster Confession says: "Man's chief end is to glorify God and to *enjoy* Him forever" [emphasis added]. Those Presbyterians of the seventeenth century understood that the chief end of man is to enjoy God.

In the greatest sermon ever preached, the Sermon on the Mount, Jesus described his followers as happy people. He taught them things like, *"Blessed* [Happy] *are they which do hunger and thirst after righteousness"* (Matthew 5:6a KJV). I know there are some who try to make the Greek word translated *blessed* mean something other than *happy,* but the Bible often uses the word *blessed* as a synonym for happiness. When the common man in Jesus' day heard the word *blessed* from the lips of Jesus, he would think of the word *happy*.

A BELIEVER'S HAPPINESS

Happiness is hard to define and much easier to describe. It is a feeling, or emotion, of intense pleasure—a sense of personal worth and of being sufficient in all things concerning life. It's the thrill in the heart of a baseball player after hitting the game-winning homerun, or the euphoria of the actor who wins the Oscar, or the intense joy in the soul of the groom who sees his bride at the back of the church waiting to walk the aisle. We know the feeling, but find it hard to define.

What boggles the mind, if we will just stop and think about it for a moment, is this: An inward state of ecstasy and joy can be in the heart of a believer regardless of circumstances. Some believe that emotions are unreliable and, as Christians, we should not pursue happiness; but Jesus, Paul, and the forefathers of the faith taught us to seek it! Further, they taught us it is possible to learn how to have inward joy regardless of our situation.

In other words, the believer can have satisfaction when he strikes out in the bottom of the ninth, is never lauded or praised, or is even abandoned by those who should love him or her.

If we know Christ and have tasted God's grace, then we are acting like unbelievers when we think our happiness is dependent upon our spouse changing, our children getting out of rebellion, or things going right at work. Happiness can be independent of our circumstances when we learn to appreciate His grace. Let me show you.

THE KEY PASSAGE (PHILIPPIANS 4)

The book of Philippians is a book about joy. As we have seen, true joy and happiness for a Christian is *independent* of our circumstances. God gives us the teaching of Paul and a personal example from Paul's life to show what it means to be happy despite one's circumstances.

Paul tells the Philippians that he is rejoicing because he finally received a long-awaited financial gift from them. They had intended to give it to him earlier but did not have the opportunity or the means. *"But I rejoiced in the Lord greatly, that now at the last your care of me has flourished again; wherein you were also careful, but you lacked opportunity"* (Philippians 4:10).

Paul was not like today's evangelists who draw salaries through a board of directors. Paul preached the gospel and received his financial support from people who were touched by his ministry. These Christians at Philippi had been supporting Paul, but, for some reason, the financial support had stopped. Maybe they had sent a messenger to give him some money, but the messenger missed Paul on his journeys. Whatever the reason, they wanted to help Paul financially but could not. They lacked the opportunity. Then somehow the opportunity came, and they were finally able to present Paul with their financial support.

Put yourself in Paul's shoes. Here he is, dependent on the gifts of others. For a long time no money had been coming in. Finally one day a messenger arrives and says, "Paul, I bring you this gift from those who love you in Philippi." So Paul sits down and writes a letter to the Philippians thanking them for their support and says, "I *rejoiced* in it."

But he does not want them to think his joy or personal happiness is dependent upon their financial generosity. He goes on to say, *"Not that I speak in respect of want"* (Philippians 4:11a). Paul is saying. "Wait, don't misunderstand. I do not rejoice or speak of my joy because my needs are now met by you financially."

And now the key statement—*"for I am content in whatever state I am."*

Do you see that Paul's joy did not have its *root* in their financial gift (although he rejoiced in it)? His joy was independent of his circumstances. *"For I have learned, in whatsoever state I am, therewith to be content"* (Philippians 4:11b KJV).

HAPPINESS IN WHAT I AM

The phrase, *"I have learned, in whatsoever state I am, therewith to be content,"* has more impact in the original Greek. The Greek literally reads *"I have learned in what I am to be self-sufficient (or content)."* In English we would say, "I am self-sufficient, or content, in who I am."

The word, *state* (or *circumstances*), is not in the original. So Paul is saying, *"I have learned in who I am to be self-sufficient (or content or happy)."* The translators supplied the word *state* (or *circumstances*) to make the verse easier to understand, and appropriately so, because if you read verse twelve, he talks about his circumstances. *"I know both how to be abased, and I know how to abound; everywhere and in all things I am instructed both to be full and to be hungry, both to abound and to suffer need"* (Philippians 4:12 KJV).

Please read carefully what Paul is saying, *"I'm grateful for your financial gift, but my joy is not dependent upon it. I don't need good circumstances to be happy. Whether I'm poor or rich, hungry or full, honored or defamed, I've learned the secret of being happy and content in 'who I am.'"*

A Crisis of Identity

Since Scripture is given for our instruction, then we, like Paul, can learn "to be content in *who I am*." This is why learning the answer to the question, *"Who am I?"* is the starting point of our search for soul satisfaction. Therefore, the million dollar question begs repeating: *"Who am I?"*

In the past, when I was asked, "Wade Burleson, *who* are you?" I would say, "I'm Wade Burleson, pastor of First Baptist Church, Holdenville, Oklahoma;" (or Emmanuel Baptist Church, Enid; or Sheridan Road Baptist Church, Tulsa.) The problem with that answer is that I am not telling people who I am; I am telling people what I do. My job is what I do, not who I am.

> We, like Paul, can learn "to be content in who I am."

Business people are like that too. When somebody asks them, "Who are you?" they tell that person what they do. The problem is that is not *who they are*.

You might look at yourself and say, "I'm a talented singer." "I'm a gifted orator." "I am a wonderful home-maker." If you begin to think of talents that you have, income that you earn, or anything that you do to answer the question, "Who are you?" then you have missed the point of the question.

You say, "Wait a minute. I'm confused. Paul says that I am to be happy in what I am. But you're telling me that I'm not to think in terms of what I do, or my talents, my relationships, my successes, my possessions, or the like to define me as a person. Then who the heck am I?" I am glad you asked.

THE GRACE OF GOD

In order for us to be happy independent of our circumstances, we must learn how to be happy in who we are as defined by the grace of God. Our contentment will come when we learn that, *"by the grace of God I am what I am"* (I Corinthians 15:10a). Our beauty, talents, successes, reputation, and relationships fade over time and ultimately go away completely. God's grace never changes.

Ladies, if somebody asks you, "Who are you?" more than likely you attach your identity to the man to whom you are married. The problem is that if your husband is not what he ought to be, then you are very unhappy because your identity is *dependent* upon him. You will then try to do everything you can to change him. When he doesn't change, you will remain one unhappy, bitter, discontented wife.

Maybe you are a mechanic, a schoolteacher, or in an occupation that is not "full-time Christian ministry." You might feel that you don't amount to much. You are not a

Billy Graham, a pastor of a church, or a missionary. You are not doing "enough" for the kingdom of God. You feel "inadequate" and "unworthy" because of what you are *not* doing. A lot of people who are in, for lack of a better term, secular work are not happy because they feel as though they ought to be doing more for God. Many believers only feel good about themselves and their relationship with God when they perceive that they are doing great things for Him.

> *Most of us get our happiness from what we do rather than who we are by the grace of God.*

Do you see that most of us get our happiness from what we do, or what others do, rather than who we are by the grace of God? If we take away all these definitions of our identity (performance, human relationships, etc.), then you might be thinking, "I don't have a clue who I am."

A Tunnel Rat

A friend of mine was a tunnel rat in Vietnam.[2] He once told me, "Pastor, nobody knows what it's like to be a tunnel rat, unless you've been there. In fact, I go back to my re-unions, to that place where all the Vietnam veterans gather, because they know what it's like."

Do you know what tunnel rats did? The Vietnamese had connecting tunnels where they kept food, bedding, and supplies. Soldiers called "tunnel rats" crawled into these tunnels, with a gun in one hand and a flashlight in the other, trying to flush out the enemy. They never knew if they would find Vietnamese at the ends of the tunnels. (The military began using dogs after too many tunnel rats were killed.)

My friend shared a story with me about coming upon his first Vietnamese who was at the end of a tunnel holding a 105-millimeter bullet. He was knocking on the end of the bullet with a hammer trying to get it to explode, to kill not only himself, but the tunnel rat as well.

He said, "You cannot imagine the fear in me. No one understands what I've been through."

As he shared his stories with me, I discovered that this Special Forces Vietnam veteran was good at what he did— very good. When he finished sharing his experiences, I asked him this question: "If I were to take away all of your honors; if I were to take away your decorations, awards, and stripes; if I were to take away all of the recognition that has come your way through what you did in Vietnam; who are you?"

I will never forget his answer. With a tear welling up in his eye, he said, "Pastor, I'm nothing. I am nothing."

I told him I appreciated his honesty. Then I showed him that the Bible agreed with his assessment of himself. II Corinthians 3:5 says, *"We are not sufficient of ourselves to think any thing of ourselves."* It was only after he came to recognize he was nothing apart from God's grace, that he said he was ready to find out what the grace of God could make him.

BE MAD—BE SAD—THEN REJOICE AND BE GLAD

You might be feeling the same pain as my friend, the tunnel rat. As you are reading this book, you might be feeling sad and thinking, "Who am I? I am nothing!"

You might even be mad at me because I have told you that the Bible says envy, credit-card debt, pride, anger, and

complaining are signs of unhappiness. I simply want you to
realize the extent of your unhappiness and the hopelessness of
your situation. I want you to become so desperate that you
cry out to God, "Help me, God, for apart from your grace I
am worse than nothing!" We need God's grace. When we
receive God's grace, we need to know what this grace does
for us.

That is what we all need to discover. We need to discover
who we are by the grace of God. Do you know the truth of
who you are by God's
grace? Do you know what

> *If you want to be happy and*
> *content, then discover the divine*
> *truth of who you are in Christ.*

God's grace has done for
you? Do you know the
grace of God? Do you feel
it in your heart? Does it invade and course through your life?
Or is it just a word in your head?

WE *CAN* BE HAPPY IN WHO WE ARE BY GOD'S GRACE

You say, "Pastor, that's too hard for me. I don't know that
I can ever answer the question, 'who am I?'" Yes, it is going
to be hard, but let me encourage you. In Philippians 4:11,
Paul says we can *learn* to be happy in who we are. The word
learn means "to unlock the mystery thereof."

We have not learned who we are in Christ because we
focus on what we are supposed to *do* or *not do*. The Bible
teaches that in Christ "I am blessed." But we think: "I am
blessed *if* I do certain things." "I am blessed *if* I am a certain
way." "I am accepted or pleasing to God *when* I meet certain
requirements or reach certain standards."

In this book, we are going to set you free from the chains of this self-oriented mindset and show you that your happiness is based upon what Christ has done for you, not in your circumstances or in your performance.

In my library is a little book written in the 1800's entitled *"Alexander on Religious Experiences."* In it he says:

> Genuine religious experience is nothing but the impression of divine truth on the mind by the energy of the Holy Spirit. There is reason to believe, therefore, that ignorance of revealed truth or error respecting it, must be attended with a corresponding defect in the religious exercises of the person.

Do you know what this means? He is saying that if you want to be happy and content, then discover the divine truth of who you are in Christ as revealed in Scripture.

If your theology is self-oriented, rather than God-oriented, you will always be struggling for happiness and contentment. You cannot be content until you learn what God is doing by His grace in your soul and life. The extent to which you have a deficient understanding of what the grace of God has done, and is doing, for you is the extent to which your happiness will be dependent on your circumstances.

UNLOCKING THE MYSTERY

Happiness does not just happen, even for believers. But Paul tells us how to unlock the mystery of happiness. It is by *learning* to be content. The "Good News" is that with the grace of God we can *learn* how to be happy despite our circumstances.

If you like to read Agatha Christie novels, you know they begin with a crime, then you try to solve "whodunit." You cannot solve or unlock the mystery until certain truths are discovered. (If you are like me, sometimes you will go to the end of the book in order to solve the mystery.) Once all of the truth is laid out, the mystery can be unlocked.

How can we *learn* happiness? The answer is simple—by finding out who we are. In the next chapters of this book, I am going to help you solve the mystery of who you are by looking at some major truths found in Scripture. We will fill in the blank in "I am ——" with the words: "I am *graced*," "I am *loved*," "I am *justified*," "I am *chosen*," "I am *blessed*," "I am *free*," "I am *protected*," "I am *adopted*," "I am *guided*," "I am *holy*," "I am *accepted*," "I am *rewarded*," and "I am *His*."

When all of this truth is laid out before you, I believe you will begin to discover who you are. You will be able to thankfully say, "I am who I am by the grace of God."

*No creature that deserved Redemption
would need to be redeemed.
They that are whole
need not the physician.*

*Christ died for men precisely because
men are **not** worth dying for;
to make them worth it.*

C.S. Lewis

Chapter 3
I Am Graced

*For by grace are ye saved through faith;
and that not of yourselves: it is the gift of God.*
Ephesians 2:8 (KJV)

I grew up in a household where I often heard the word *grace*. I've been in churches all my life where the word *grace* is frequently used in sermons, Sunday School lessons, and songs. We get so accustomed to the word *grace* that we lose appreciation for the concept of that word.

Several years ago, a friend of mine moved to Florida to pastor a church. He grew up in the Bible Belt singing the great hymn "Amazing Grace" almost every Sunday. When he got to Florida, he found out that the young people knew "Amazing Grace" simply as the *Silkwood* song. The critically acclaimed movie on the life of Karen Silkwood, starring Cher, closes with a soulful rendition of "Amazing Grace." We are living in a nation where young people know this great song by going to the movies rather than going to church!

Since that is the case, we need to examine the concept of grace. Then we must ask ourselves two questions:

1. Does God grace the undeserving?
2. Has God graced me?

DEFINING GRACE

I have a hard time defining *grace* because the Bible gives no definition of grace. The Bible *describes* grace but does not *define* it.

Some define grace in the form of an acrostic, *G.R.A.C.E.* — "GOD'S RICHES AT CHRIST'S EXPENSE." Others define grace as "unmerited favor." The dictionary defines grace as simply "favor or kindness."

Grace is generally used as a noun. In the context of our search for identity, the question, "Am I graced?" means, "Have I received the grace of God?"

POSITIVE *DE*-MERIT

A.W. Pink attempted to define the grace of God in a book entitled *The Sovereignty of God*. He had a friend read the manuscript before he sent it to the publisher. Pink explains how his friend helped him define grace in a better manner:

> An esteemed friend who kindly read through this book in its manuscript form, and to whom we are indebted for a number of excellent suggestions, has pointed out that, grace is something more than "unmerited favor." To feed a tramp who calls on me is "unmerited favor," but it is scarcely grace. But suppose that after robbing me I should feed this starving tramp—that would be "grace." Grace, then, is favor shown where there is positive *de*-merit in the one receiving it.

Read carefully—*grace is favor shown those with positive* de-*merit*. "Merited" favor is given to a person who earns it. "Unmerited" favor is given to one who is unable to do anything to earn it. But "positive *de*-merit" is found in the one who not only does not deserve favor, but who is also guilty of committing a crime against the one bestowing favor.

Grace would not be grace unless the person receiving it had "*de*-merit" in him. Unless a person is positively unworthy and undeserving of the favor being given to him, it cannot be called grace.

GRACE IS NOT OBLIGATION

Favor given to the worthy is not grace—it is obligation. We are obliged to give favor to the person who earns it. We are obliged to give blessing to the person who deserves it.

If I agree to work for you and complete the tasks assigned to me, at the end of the day you will pay me my wages. It is your obligation. You owe me my wages because I have earned them. You would be unjust if you didn't pay me.

> &
> *Grace is favor shown to those with positive de-merit.*
> &

On the other hand, if I am given responsibilities and I cast them to the wind, shirk my duty, thumb my nose at my obligations, then you do not owe me a cent. Frankly, if I shirk my obligations under an agreement with you, then you have the right to punish me for my neglect of duty.

So it is with God. Paul said, *"Now to him that works is the reward not reckoned of grace, but of debt"* (Romans 4:4). If God favored us because of our good works, then His favor would have to be called an obligation, or a duty. It would not be called grace.

NONE OF US DESERVE GRACE

Mankind was given responsibility in the garden of Eden. Man was in an agreement with God to love Him, honor Him, and obey Him. Man shirked his duty. God has punished all of humankind because of the sin of one man, Adam.

There is no way we can now earn the favor of God. All of us, because of Adam and our own personal sins against God, have *de*-merit toward Him. *None of us deserve the favor and blessing of God.*

GOD IS UNDER NO OBLIGATION TO FAVOR ANY ONE

Those of us who have grown up in churches simply *assume* God is gracious to everyone. We assume this because it is what we have been told. We sing songs like, "Jesus loves the little children, all the children of the world," and just know in our hearts that God graces every single human being.

However, the Bible makes it very clear that there will be people in hell. The Bible is abundantly precise about the fact that there are people who will bear the wrath of a holy God for eternity.

Why are people in hell? They are in hell because they deserve it. Short and simple—they have earned it. It is deserved and earned by all of us because of our choices. Because we have freely and willingly rebelled against our Creator, we are bound to the chains of eternal justice. We will see in Chapter Five that every one of us deserves God's wrath because of Adam's sin, as well as our own multiple personal sins.

GOD IS RIGHT—OUR CULTURE IS WRONG

Not one person in hell will accuse God of injustice. There will not be one tear shed by the relatives of those in hell over God's injustice. God is a righteous, just God. That means He does things right!

Paul asks the question, *"Is God unrighteous who takes vengeance? (I speak as a man.) God forbid!"* (Romans 3:5b-6a). God never does anything that is not right, just, holy, and as it ought to be.

In our day, the very idea that God could send somebody to hell as a just punishment for sin is really old-fashioned. In fact, our culture flaunts open disdain for God's laws. The possibility that God would punish someone for violating His law doesn't even flicker across the fires of conscience today.

Adultery, self-gratification, drunkenness, homosexuality, pride, cursing God's name, lying, stealing, bitterness, envy, and every other violation of God's standard is considered not only the *norm*—it is now *cool!*

Jonathan Edwards and Hell

This is nothing new! Jonathan Edwards faced a similar situation during his days of preaching throughout the New England Colonies in the early 1700's. This graduate of Yale was called to be the pastor of First Church, Northampton, Massachusetts, in 1729. When he began his ministry in Northampton, the bars were full and the churches were empty. People had no concern for the eternal nature of their souls. As a result, Jonathan Edwards prepared many sermons on the condition of the wicked and, in particular, their final judgment. The following is from the message "Final Judgment" preached by Jonathan Edwards on the text Romans 2:8,9 as he sought to describe the awful predicament of the person without God's grace (emphasis mine).

Every one of mankind must have the portion that belongs to him. God allots to each one his portion; and *the portion of the wicked is nothing but wrath, and distress, and anguish of soul.* Though they may enjoy a few empty and vain pleasures and delights, for a few days while they stay in this world, *yet that which is allotted to them by the Possessor and Governor of all things to be their portion, is only indignation and wrath, tribulation and anguish.*

This is not the portion that wicked men choose; the portion that they choose is worldly happiness, yet it is the portion that God carves out for them; it is the portion that they in effect choose for themselves. For they choose those things that naturally and necessarily lead to it, and those that they are plainly told, times without number, will issue in it.

Proverbs. 8:36 *"But he that sins against me, wrongs his own soul; all they that hate me love death."* But whether they choose it or not, this will and must be the portion to all eternity of all who live and die wicked men. Indignation and wrath shall pursue them as long as they live in this world, shall drive them out of the world, and shall follow them into another world; and there wrath and misery shall abide upon them throughout eternity.

This kind of preaching was used by God to bring people to a sense of hopelessness and despair. It led to a revival that swept the New England coast, which historians call "The Great Awakening."

DESPERATE SINNERS

All of us are guilty before God. We can't do a thing to rid ourselves of this guilt. God has every right to damn us for eternity and pour out His wrath upon us not only after this life, but during this life as well. We *are* desperate sinners!

C. S. Lewis says, "The Christian religion is, in the long run, a thing of unspeakable comfort. But it does not begin in comfort; it begins in . . . dismay . . . it is no use at all trying to go on to that comfort without first going through that dismay."[1]

I want to make a statement that is critical to our search for soul significance—*Every person deserves hell, and God has every right to send every person to hell.*

Why is the above statement so crucial? Because once we

> ❧
> *If there were no bad news,*
> *there would be no good news.*
> ❧

realize that God has every right to damn us; and once we realize there is nothing we can do to bring ourselves up out of the miry pit of sin and condemnation, then we are ready for the good news.

Good news is only good when there is the knowledge of bad news. If there were no bad news, there would be no good news.

GOD HAS CHOSEN TO GRACE A SPECIFIC NUMBER OF SINNERS

But God (D. M. Lloyd-Jones says *but God* are the two greatest words in the Bible), in His infinite wisdom and plan for the universe has chosen to show grace (favor to the undeserving) to a people whom He has loved even before the foundation of the world.

These people are called several things in Scripture such as: *"His people"* (Matthew 1:21) as compared to those *"He never knew* [loved]" (Matthew 7:23); *"the bride of Christ"* (Revelation 22:17) as compared to *"the harlot"* (Revelation 17:5); *"saints"* (Ephesians 1:1) as compared to *"reprobates"* (II Corinthians 13:5); and *"my sheep"* (John 10:14) as compared to *"the goats"* (Matthew 25:32). I could go on and on with comparisons.

The point is that God has chosen to favor a multitude of sinners that no man can number, from every tribe, race, kindred, and family—from the entire world (Revelation 5:9). This grace is given *because* of His love for those unworthy sinners whom He *chooses* to grace.

In addition to being holy, God is loving. He chooses to love for the praise of His grace. He chooses to condemn for the praise of His holiness. Grace could never be present unless holiness and judgment were just as real as love and salvation.

WHO ARE THESE GRACED INDIVIDUALS?

We won't fully know who these graced individuals are until we get to heaven. God knows His sheep by name, and He has guaranteed that all of them will be saved! Jesus said, *"All that the Father gives me shall come to me; and him that comes to me I will not cast out . . . of all which he has given me I should lose nothing, but should raise it up again at the last day"* (John 6: 37-39).

The big question is "Am I graced?" How do I know whether or not the favor of God abides upon me?

First, I must see myself as a desperate sinner, full of demerit, and not worthy of God's favor. Christ is not a physician to those who see themselves as whole, but He has come to heal those who know themselves to be in need of a physician (Luke 5:31,32). Only grace allows us to humbly admit our condition.

Pride will not allow a person to say he is deserving of God's wrath. Pride is the natural condition of the human heart. Only God's favor humbles us and brings us to the conclusion that if God chose not to forgive us, He would be just and righteous.

Second, our faith in Christ is the evidence of God's favor. *"Kiss the Son, lest He be angry,"* says the Psalmist (Psalm 2:12). The holy anger, wrath, and judgment of God abide with those who will never trust in the person and work of Christ. Believers in Jesus Christ are the only ones who have the warrant to believe that they are favored by God, despite their demerit and unworthiness, because they have trusted in the very Person who delivered them from what they deserve— God's wrath.

GRACE PRECEDES FAITH

Faith in Christ is the evidence of God's favor, but this faith can be difficult to explain. In his powerful sermon, *"Dei Gratia,"* which he delivered in 1870, C. H. Spurgeon explained faith this way:

> Often as we explain faith, yet still we need to explain it again. I met with an illustration taken from the American war. One had been trying to instruct a dying officer in what faith was. At last he caught the idea, and he said, 'I could not understand it before, but I see it now. It is just this-I *surrender,* I surrender to Jesus.' That is it. You have been fighting against God, standing out against him, trying to make terms more or less favourable to yourself; now here you stand in the presence of God, and you drop the sword of your rebellion and say, 'Lord, I surrender, I am thy prisoner. I trust to thy mercy to save me. I have done with self, I fall into thy arms.'

C. S. Lewis in describing his conversion says, "Total surrender, the absolute leap in the dark, were demanded. . . . The demand was not even "All or nothing." . . . the demand was simply 'All.'" [2]

Surrender is to give up possession, or power, over. Surrender is to yield. All that is required of us is to lay down the arms of our self-righteousness and, by faith, surrender to the God of all grace.

Our faith in Christ is a gift of God's grace. *"For by grace are you saved through faith; and that not of yourselves; it is the gift of God"* (Ephesians 2:8). Our faith is the evidence of, not the reason for, God's favor. God's favor is the reason for our faith. If God has given His Son to die for us, then He will surely give us the necessary faith to believe in the Savior.

Nobody seeks after God. *"There is no one that seeks God"* (Romans 3:11). Jesus Christ is tasteless to the man without grace. Those upon whom the favor of God does not fall find Christ to be "moronic" (the literal translation of the Greek word *foolishness* in I Corinthians 2:14). But those upon whom the favor of God falls find Christ to be the One who quenches their thirst and satisfies their hunger. We fall in love with God because He first loved us and gave His Son for us.

HOW DID GOD SHOW HIS LOVE TO SINNERS?

In love, God sent His Son, Jesus, from heaven. He, and He alone, lived a life that merited God's favor.

When He died on the cross of Calvary, He died as a sinner, as one with demerit, because He took our sins and demerit upon Himself. When Jesus Christ died on Calvary, He stood in our stead; He

> *Nothing could have brought Jesus from the throne of glory to the cross of woe, but grace.*

stretched his arms in our stead; He received the thorns in our stead, the spear in His side in our stead. He bore our sin and guilt upon Himself, so that the anger and wrath of God due us as desperate sinners became His. He who knew no sin became sin for us. When He cried out, "It is finished!" the price was paid in full for our salvation. The wrath of God was poured out—the justice of God due His people was satisfied.

Why did Christ die for sinners? C. H. Spurgeon in *"Dei Gratia"* explains: "Nothing could have brought him from the throne of glory to the cross of woe but grace, unalloyed, unbounded grace."

WHAT CAN WE DO?

You might ask, "Don't we contribute anything to our salvation?" Scripture answers, "Yes, our sin."[3]

Nothing that we do can contribute one thing to our salvation, no matter how hard we try. Charles Swindoll says, "There is one and only one password for entering heaven: Grace." [4]

We think that if we live up to certain standards, we will merit God's favor. We think we must do certain things to receive God's grace. But it is not what we do. It is not what we commit. It is not our religion. It is not our baptism.

I know firsthand how we often deceive people into thinking they must *do* something to receive grace. We tell people that they must walk an aisle, pray a "sinner's prayer," or make a commitment to Christ. Then we tell them if they want to receive the rest of the gifts of grace, if they want to be truly blessed, then they must meet more standards and follow more disciplines—have a regular devotional time, attend church regularly, live a holy life. If they perform to these standards, God will give them more grace. We teach that they must have some merit, that they must do their part.

My wife makes beautiful patchwork quilts. She skillfully mixes a piece of one fabric here and a piece of another fabric there, and the different pieces come together to form one quilt. But that is not how it is with grace. Spurgeon says it is no

> *Grace is no patchwork of human merit here and God's grace there.*

patchwork of human merit here and God's grace there. It is God and God alone from first to last. *"Salvation is of the Lord"* (Jonah 2:9b).

GROWING IN GRACE

We can't contribute anything to our salvation, but we can grow in grace. A believer grows in grace the same way a child grows in nature. We grow spiritually in much the the same way as we grow physically. This book is designed to help you grow in grace.

Those of you, like my wife and me, who have children know that when Mom prepares a meal, the kids gather around the table and eat. As a result, they will grow physically.

A believer grows in grace, grows spiritually, as he comes to the table where God's word has been prepared. He partakes of it, and it becomes his. He swallows it. He meditates upon it. He thinks on it. Is it any wonder that the psalmist said, *"How sweet are your words unto my taste"* (Psalm 119:103a)? Notice, he didn't say thy words are sweet unto my *hearing*. The psalmist said, "Your words are sweet unto my *taste*."

Growing in grace is a process of feasting on the word of God and trusting in what He says about us—graced sinners who have looked to Christ for deliverance.

OTHER GIFTS OF GRACE

As we grow in grace, we will find that God has not only given His Son to die for us, He has not only given us the necessary faith to believe in the Savior; but also all other gifts of grace that make life exciting. Spurgeon says, "It must be grace that makes the dead soul live, but it is equally grace that keeps the living soul alive."

If God delivered His Son for us—and He did for all those who will believe—then what will He not give us in things relating to Christ? Will He withhold blessings? No. Will He withhold answers to our prayers? No. Will He withhold divine guidance? No. Will He withhold any gift of grace? No.

When it comes to our salvation, we are in good hands with God. If Christ died for us, then everything associated with Jesus Christ will be freely given to us.

Imagine you have a teenage son who dies unexpectedly. The doctors come to you and ask if you will donate your son's organs to those awaiting transplants. You agree, and one person receives his heart, another his lungs, his kidneys, corneas, and so forth.

Then imagine that a few years go by and your doorbell rings. A young adult stands at your door and says, "You don't know me, but I'm the one who received the gift of life from your son. Your son's heart beats within my chest. May I come in?"

"Of course," you would say. If that young person said, "Can you tell me about your son?" would you deny him anything about your son? Would you not share with him everything else associated with your son?

Yes, you would because you have already given him the difficult part. In the same way, if we are believers, God, who has given us His Son, will by His grace freely give us all the gifts associated with His grace. *"How shall he not with Him also freely give us all things?"* (Romans 8:32).

In the rest of the chapters of this book, we will see all the gifts associated with grace. We will see that these gifts have already been received by those who believe. As we look at these gifts, we will find that, in Christ, we have all we need to live happy and contented lives.

It all begins with "I am graced." Can you say, "I am graced"? Is your trust in Jesus Christ as your Lord and Savior? Have you surrendered all to Him? Do you see that you have no hope apart from Christ?

The grace of God is the beginning of true happiness.

*Nothing is more evident than
that God's choosing
His people in Christ before
the foundation of the world,
is an act of love;
and I will venture to say,
it is an act of love,
founded upon, and springing from
his delight in them.*

John Gill

Chapter 4
I Am Loved

We love Him because He first loved us.
I John 4:19

I will never forget the pain and grief in the hearts of a mother and father who had called me to their home. Their son was about to be arrested for gross sexual misconduct. I will never forget the tears, the weeping, the agony over what their boy had done, which had harmed dozens of people.

I will also never forget what that father, a friend of mine, said to his son. He called the boy over to him and said, "Son, I want you to know I love you regardless of your behavior." Then he caught the boy up in an affectionate embrace.

The son melted into tears. He broke down, he wept, he cried out, "But Dad, I don't deserve it! I don't deserve your love."

His dad replied, "Son, I love you because of what I have invested in you. You're my boy."

If we know Christ, God loves us because we are His child. No matter what happens in our lives, *"neither height, nor depth, nor principalities or powers, not one single thing can separate us from the love of God, which is found in Christ Jesus"* (Romans 8:38-39).

Am I Loved?

Like my friends' son, believers do not always fully understand the love of God for them. We will say, "God loves me," but in the same breath we will say, "God is frustrated with me, and disappointed in me, and angry with me." That is a faulty understanding of God's love built on a belief that God loves us as other human beings love us.

In this chapter we are going to examine the unconditional love of God for the believer. We are going to discover that one of the foundational answers to the question of "Who am I?" is "I am loved."

This is not going to be a generic Bible study on God's love for the world. I am speaking of God's peculiar, distinguishing love for His people—believers, the church, the elect, whatever you want to call them. Those apart from Christ cannot have true happiness. They may be happy for a season but it will fade over time. Those who are in Christ can learn to rest in a deep happiness and contentment, no matter the circumstances, because they discover that they are loved by God eternally.

What Is Love?

Love is defined as a strong feeling of affection, pleasure, and tender attachment. When I say that God loves his people I mean exactly this: God has for His people a strong feeling of affection, pleasure, and tender attachment.

In the Greek language (the language of the New Testament), there are four words for love: *phileo,* meaning brotherly love or friendship; *eros,* meaning romantic or sexual love; *storge,* meaning tender love or affection; and *agape,* meaning benevolent love (which the King James Bible translates as charity). God's love for His people is *agape* love—a warm, kind, charitable, eternal love.

THE LOVE OF GOD

Agape **love is not conditional love.** As humans, most of our experiences in the area of love have been based upon conditional love. We feel that someone takes pleasure in us, has affection for us, or desires an attachment with us when we are lovely. Conditional love is love that rises or falls due to the lovableness of the one being loved. That is the kind of love the world has.

We might say, "I love my dog." But if that dog gets fleas, or starts tearing up the furniture, or eating our socks, our love for him flies out the window.

When two people meet, they say that they "fall in love." Why do they do that? It is because the other person, the opposite sex, the future spouse, is lovely in the eye of the beholder. So they fall in love. A feeling of attachment, affection, or pleasure arises within the heart.

Then they get married. Over time, the one whom they used to perceive as lovely is not as lovely as they once thought. They develop circles around the eyes, and more circles move to around the middle. Those things that used to be cute are now irritating. Those things that they used to laugh at, they now complain about. Eventually, they find themselves in the pastor's office for counseling. They say, "Pastor, I don't know what the problem is. I just don't love so-and-so like I used to." That is what happens with conditional love.

Agape **love is unconditional love.** Unconditional love is a strong feeling of affection, pleasure, and tender attachment that is due to *the nature of the one loving*, rather than *the one being loved*.

Unconditional love means that we love, take pleasure in, and have fond feelings for a person, regardless of how lovely he or she is, because *our* nature is such that we can love that way.

God's love for His people is always unconditional. God's love for His people is due to the nature of God, rather than the worthiness of the one being loved. *"God is love"* (I John 4:8). Alexander McClaren says, "God's love is not drawn out by our lovableness; but wells up, like an artesian spring, from the depths of His nature."

John Blanchard said, "God loved us when there was nothing good to be seen in us and nothing good to be said for us."[1] God did not look down on us as lovable. He did not look down and see us as ones who would bring Him pleasure. He looked down and saw sinners in rebellion toward Him, at enmity, at odds with Him; but He loved us.

> God loved us when there was nothing good to be seen in us and nothing good to be said for us.

There is a mistaken notion among some that God hated us, so He sent His Son Jesus Christ; and then Jesus convinced the Father to love us by dying for us. But the truth is, God loved us even while we were yet sinners (Romans 5:8). He chose to love us because of who He is. He gave His Son to die in our stead because of His love for us as sinners whom He sovereignly chose to love.

God's love for His people is eternal. In his book, *The Knowledge of the Holy*, A. W. Tozer says this about the love of God:

> From God's other known attributes we may learn much about His love. We can know, for instance, that because God is self-existent, His love had no beginning; because He is eternal, His love can have no end; because it is infinite, it has no limit.[2]

God reminds us through the Old Testament prophet Jeremiah that, *"I have loved you with an everlasting love"* (Jeremiah 31:3b). Many of the promises in the Old Covenant (which are found in the Old Testament) were for Old Covenant Israel and were conditional. However, God, in His grace, chose to give those living under the Old Covenant some refreshing glimpses of His unconditional love.

References to the unconditional love of God are found throughout the Old Testament. The Hebrew word *hesed* is used over two hundred times in the Old Testament. It is a unique combination of loyalty, righteousness, and love often translated as *lovingkindness*. *Hesed* is a special word used to designate the covenant love that God has for His people. In the book of Hosea, the word *hesed* illustrates God's faithful love for His unfaithful people (Hosea 2:19). When we see God's love reaching back so far into the past, we can be assured it has no limit in the future.

God's love for His people is personal. When we talk about the love of God, we have a tendency to talk about how God loves the whole, wide world. But what we need to see is how we, personally and individually, are loved by God. God's feelings of tender attachment, pleasure, and affection are toward me as a person. His love is toward Wade, it is toward John, and Mary, and Tom, and so on.

One of the reasons we have never learned to be content and happy in whatever state we are in (Philippians 4:11) is because the love of God is only something we know in our heads—not in our hearts. If we experientially know the love of God, if we feel it, rest in it, and revel in it; then we will not need the love of anyone else to bring us fulfillment and contentment. We can be content even when everyone else turns against us.

God loved *me,* and because He could not just forgive me without violating His justice, He sent His Son to pay the price for my sin on a cursed cross. Never forget, it is God's love that compelled Him to come to earth and die for His people. God's love for me precedes everything else. I know that He loves me because I have embraced His Son. You, too, may know that God has chosen to love you when you love His Son. He does not love the people who do not love his Son (Psalm 2:12).

GOD SEARCHES AND KNOWS ME

In the Psalms, David, a graced sinner, writes of his experience with the unconditional love of God. He says, *"O Lord, thou hast searched me and known me"* (Psalm 139:1 KJV). The word *searched,* in the original language, has the idea of one who diligently probes or takes a light and shines it in dark places to search for something.

I wear contact lenses. Once I dropped one down the sink. I got a flashlight and diligently probed the darkness of that slimy drainpipe searching for my contact. That is what the

Lord does to us. He probes us, He diligently searches us, and He knows us.

My wife knows me better than anyone. She has seen my faults, my weaknesses, and my sins. But she has not probed me and searched me like God has. He has searched me, and He knows me. He knows when my motivation is selfish. He knows when the word on my tongue is evil, even if I do not communicate it. He knows my heart, my character, my attitudes, my intentions, and my motivations. This could cause me to have great fear because the more I know about me, the more I realize how defiled is the heart of Wade Burleson.

> *Thou knowest my downsitting and mine uprising, thou understandest my thought afar off. Thou compassest my path and my lying down, and art acquainted with all my ways. For there is not a word in my tongue, but, lo, O Lord, thou knowest it altogether. Thou hast beset me behind and before, and laid thine hand upon me. Such knowledge is too wonderful for me; it is high, I cannot attain unto* [fathom] *it.* (Psalm 139:2-6 KJV)

How would you like it if people knew you the way David has just described God knowing him? How would you like it if all of your secrets were exposed? How would you feel if everything you thought suddenly were an expressed word? Everyone around you knew it, and knew that it came from your mouth, your heart, your mind.

I would blush. My church would fire me. You know why? Because some of my hidden motives are corrupt. Even though I am honest enough to say that, I still hide them really well—and you hide them really well—from others. But we do not hide them from God.

WE CANNOT HIDE FROM GOD

So what do we do? We only have the experience of conditional love from others. When conditional love exists and our sins are exposed, we want to flee. When we see how well God knows us, and when we know what is deep inside ourselves, then we want to flee from God and hide from His presence. But where can we go?

> *Whither shall I flee from thy presence? If I ascend up into heaven, thou art there; if I make my bed in hell, behold thou art there. If I take the wings of the morning, and dwell in the uttermost parts of the sea; even there shall thy hand lead me, and thy right hand shall hold me. If I say, Surely the darkness shall cover me; even the night shall be light about me. Yea, the darkness hideth not from thee; but the night shineth as the day; the darkness and the light are both alike to thee.*
> (Psalm 139:7-12 KJV)

I can just imagine David as he writes this saying, "Lord, you know me that well? I want to hide. I want to run! You know me better than I know myself. I hide from people who know me. You know me better than they do. I want to hide from you!" David wants to hide because he cannot fathom the knowledge of God's unconditional love.

GOD'S THOUGHTS TOWARD US

This desire to run from God and hide from Him is a sign that we do not understand the nature of His love. We have not learned the truth about God's opinion of us. The only thing that will keep us from running and hiding from God is to learn what David learned about God's love. David says, *"How precious also are thy thoughts unto me, O God! How great is the sum of them!"* (Psalm 139:17 KJV).

The word *precious* is literally the word *rare*. The word *rare* can mean "few in number," or it can mean "different in nature."

If a person should happen to find a lunar rock, it would be rare because no one else has one—only governments. He would be the only private citizen to possess a rock from the moon. It would be valuable because it is "rare in number." Were God's thoughts for David rare in number? No. Because David says, "How *great* is the sum of" your thoughts unto me.

If not rare in number, then God's thoughts for David and His people must be rare because they are "different in nature." The air above our atmosphere is rare because it is different than the air that surrounds us. Likewise God's thoughts toward His covenant people, believers, are rare. They are rare because they are different in nature. His love for us is different in nature than human love, which is conditional. His love for David, for believers, for all His people, is the rare, unconditional, agape love that flows from God's heart because of who He is.

> *Agape love flows from God's heart because of who He is.*

WE ARE FREE TO STOP HIDING

When we begin to understand that we are loved that way, we can stop hiding. If God loves us like that, then we can be open and honest to other people about our faults, our failures, our motives, and our intentions.

We do not mind when somebody corrects us, criticizes us, or calls us into question. We know ourselves and know that we have failings, but we also know there is One who loves us. There is no need to get defensive. We do not have to try to prove that we are okay. We do not need to act as if we have no weaknesses. We can be open and honest and say, "Yes, I see. You're right. But isn't it good that God loves me in the midst of my weakness?"

Moreover, when we finally understand God's unconditional love for us, it can free us up to have that kind of love for others.

WHAT ABOUT UNBELIEVERS?

We must be careful, again, to be biblical in our concept of God's love. Even though it is hard for us to understand, and harder yet to accept, the Bible teaches that God's unconditional love is only reserved for His covenant people. This kind of love is set aside for believers only. God does not love those who reject His Son in the same way He loves those who embrace His Son.

We have no warrant to say to anyone that God loves him or her unconditionally until we see evidence of God's grace, which is faith in Jesus Christ. We can only say to the unbeliever, "if you do not 'kiss the Son,' God is angry" (Psalm 2:12).

If you are not one of His people right now, if you do not have assurance that He is your Lord and Savior, the invitation of the gospel is clear—whosoever will, may come.

We do not have to change in order to be loved. *He* changes His children. We must "kiss the Son"; embrace the Christ. The wrath of God for us dissipated at Calvary because of the death of Jesus Christ. The grace of God transforms the lives of all those who "kiss the Son."

Leighton Ford said, "The reality of God's wrath is as much a part of the biblical message as is God's grace." *"God is angry with the wicked every day"* (Psalm 7:11b). This should create a desire in us to take the gospel to every person. We are to bring Jesus to every sinner. This is why Jesus commissioned us to go and share the gospel (Matthew 28:19-20).

ISN'T FAITH A CONDITION?

You might say, "Then isn't that a condition—that you must believe?" Faith in Christ is not a *condition* for God to love us. It is the *evidence* that he has set His love upon us. God loves people as sinners, and faith in Christ is a gift of His love.

NOTHING CAN REMOVE HIS LOVE FOR US

Some think outward circumstances are evidence of God's love. When they see health and prosperity in the life of a believer, they think that is a sure sign of God's love and favor. If they see suffering in the life of a believer, they think that is evidence of fleeing love. But nothing separates us from the love of God.

> *Who shall separate us from the love of Christ? Shall tribulation, or distress, or persecution, or famine or nakedness, or peril or sword? . . . For I am persuaded, that neither death nor life, nor angels, nor principalities, nor powers, nor things present, nor things to come, nor height, nor depth, nor any other creature, shall be able to separate us from the love of God, which is in Christ Jesus our Lord.* (Romans 8:35, 38-39 KJV)

When God sets His love upon us, there is not a single thing that can remove it. Neither death, nor life, nor anything can separate us from His love. When we are saved by the grace of God, we are forever saved.

THEN WHY DO GOOD WORKS?

If nothing can remove His love for us, then we might wonder why we should do good works. You might say, "If I believe that God's love is upon me, if I can have assurance that He set His affection upon me, then I'm afraid I will lose my motivation for being obedient and doing good."

This is the argument that is usually given to me about eternal security. "If I believed in eternal security, I would have no motivation for living a godly life."

Do you mean to tell me that the New Covenant evangelical motive for doing good, or being obedient, is fear of punishment, or loss of God's love? It is the reverse. Good works are our response to His unconditional love, not our efforts to obtain His love.

WHAT ABOUT SIN?

If nothing separates us from the love of God, then it seems as if we would just feel free to go out and sin however we like. But I have found that those who most understand the love of God are the least likely to sin. The more they see His love for them, the more they love and obey Him. When they experience unconditional love, they respond with love that wells up within them for Him because of how He loved them. *"We love Him because He first loved us"* (I John 4:19).

> *Those who most understand the love of God are the least likely to sin.*

The goodness of God is what leads to repentance. Those who want to hear the wrath and anger of God to keep themselves from sinning are those whose hearts have never been changed. They are living under the law—the Old Covenant. Their motivation is to avoid God's anger. They have never learned what it means to be a New Covenant believer. The Old Covenant said, "Do this and live." The New Covenant says, "Christ did all that is required for us to live!"

The evidence of God's love is faith in Christ and repentance of sin. Absence of sin is not what proves us to be children of God, because the children of God struggle with sin. But if, when confronted with our sin, we are broken and we hurt, then we know God's Spirit resides within us. We know we have done wrong and will confess and forsake it. Those who profess to be children of God, but love to continue in sin (I John), are not truly children of God. They are illegitimate.

THE GOSPEL

The gospel, at its very core, promises that no matter how vile a sinner I am, if I, by the grace of God, simply see Christ as the Savior for sinners and cling to Him, then I have received God's grace. That is the gospel. That is the love of God.

When we begin to truly comprehend the unconditional love of God for us, then we begin to love Him. We begin to love the things about Him. We love His word. We love to come to church and worship Him. Our soul longs to worship the God who loves us.

The unconditional love that is part of God's nature can become a part of our nature, and we can extend that love to others. We will be compassionate and forgiving because we know how much compassion and forgiveness we have received from God. If we have a neighbor, friend, family member, or spouse without Jesus Christ, we do not feel superior to them. We know we have not obtained the love of God because we are somehow more spiritual, more religious, or more holy than others. We know the love of God for us wells up within Him like an artesian spring and is not drawn from Him because of our loveliness—we are not lovely.

Until we understand how steadfastly, unconditionally, and deeply we are loved by God, we can never truly love others. If God's unconditional love is difficult for you to accept and understand, be patient. I believe as you go through the remaining "I am ——" chapters in this book, things will begin to click in your mind. As you add to the truths of who you are in Christ, you will be overwhelmed by His grace.

They [sinners] *are justified*
by the obedience and blood of Christ,
cleared of all charges,
acquitted and absolved,
and freed from all condemnation
and death and given eternal life.

John Gill

Chapter 5
I Am Justified

Being justified freely by His grace
through the redemption that is in Christ Jesus.
Romans 3:24 (KJV)

I have a dear friend who studied to be a priest. He went to seminary in order to learn the doctrine of his church. While there, he learned a great many things. One thing that troubled him was the teaching that a person should strive to live his life completely perfect before God.

He really tried but would often fail. It bothered him that he failed to live a perfect priest's life, but what really tortured him was how he could be made right with God after he failed. He had a hard time seeing how God could take delight in him since God was so holy and his sin was an offense to God's great character.

His church told him to do certain things—say certain prayers, light a few candles, confess, and do works of penance, but there was this nagging notion in the back of his head that went something like this:

"How can God like me when I fail so much? Does he not get tired of forgiving me?"

Have you ever felt like God is tired of you? Have you made many promises to God to reform your bad behavior, only to break those promises and feel that God then wants nothing to do with you?

My friend went to his superiors who sought to convince him that through his use of the sacraments and sincere repentance of his sins, God's forgiveness would be granted. This, though, did not solve my friend's problem. It was not enough to know that God forgave him—*he needed to know that God took great delight and pleasure in him*.

He once asked his superior how he would feel if a neighbor borrowed the church's tools, promising to return them, only to show up day after day, apologizing for losing yesterday's tools, but asking for more tools? Would not the church say to the neighbor—"get lost?" That is how my friend thought God felt about him—"get lost!"

A GREAT GIFT

One of God's gifts for believers in Jesus Christ is justification. This wonderful grace gift answers the question of how and why God delights in people who know themselves to be sinners and why He refuses to say to Christians "get lost!" In this chapter, we will see what justification is, how justification is different from being forgiven by God, and why it is so much more wonderful and powerful than our feeble attempts to become pleasing to God by what we do.

Remember my priest friend's nagging question: *"How can God enjoy my company if I am a forgiven sinner? I'm still sinful and He is holy. He may forgive me, but He doesn't like me since I'm not perfect."*

My friend rightly discerned that God demanded perfection from him. None of this halfhearted, halftime obedience. Jesus said, *"Be perfect even as my Father in heaven is perfect"* (Matthew 5:48). Everyone will give an account to Him as to how they measure up to His law. Coming close doesn't count. Full obedience is the standard—God accepts nothing less. Not one of us measures up.

Unfortunately, churches are full of people who pretend they *do* measure up. The Pharisees in Jesus' day thought they measured up, and the religious Pharisees of today feel they measure up—and others don't. Religious activity is often motivated by the desire for God's approval and acceptance. When will we learn that all of our obedience is never without the taint of sin? And when will we also learn that we need *more* than forgiveness from God to be in fellowship with Him?

BEING GOOD IS NOT GOOD ENOUGH

This is where God's gift of justification to believers becomes so important! Our justification is what allows God to welcome us with gladness into His presence, and allows Him one day to receive us with joy into His heavenly home. It is not because we are pardoned, but because *He justifies us!* He delights in our company and enjoys our communion with Him because He considers us perfectly righteous and perfectly holy before Him.

> *To be justified by God is a much greater thing than to be forgiven by God.*

Pardon is the removal of punishment for the guilty. Justification is a declaration that a person is completely righteous and obedient to God's law and, therefore, deserving of God's countless blessings. *To be justified by God is a much greater thing than to be forgiven by God.*

In Christ we are not only pardoned, we are justified. *We can't justify ourselves before God.* It is impossible. The damage has been done. We *are* guilty before God; we deserve His condemnation. Our righteous acts, if presented to God to convince God to like us, are like filthy rags before a holy God (Isaiah 64:6).

Being good in our own eyes and in the eyes of men is not good enough. God's character and majestic holiness demands absolute perfection before there can be fellowship with Him.

This is why we need to be justified *by God*—because we can't do it ourselves! You and I stand guilty before the Judge of heaven and earth.

TELL ME THE BAD NEWS FIRST

The gospel (which means *good news*) is only appreciated when people know the bad news. Has anyone ever asked you, "I've got good news and bad news. Which do you want to hear first?" I always choose to hear the bad news first! Why? Because the good news is *really* good when it follows the bad news.

So, let me give you the bad news. The Bible declares that all of us are guilty before God because of someone else's sin—Adam's sin. Oh, sure, if we were honest before God, we would freely admit that we deserve His condemnation for our own sins, but the Bible says God judges us for another person's sin! Our personal sins only greatly compound our rightful condemnation and confirm our sinfulness before

God. We all deserve God's punishment. You, I, the Pope, John Calvin, Mother Teresa, Billy Graham, and anybody else you want to name deserve condemnation because of our sins. *Yet we are condemned even without our personal sins because of Adam's sin.* That's the bad news.

Therefore, if we could live our lives and never sin against God, He *would still* condemn us because of another person's sin (Adam's). We are guilty in Adam, and can't do anything to justify ourselves. This is why there is no such thing as the "age of accountability." Everyone is condemned because of one man's sin.

FEDERAL REPRESENTATION

The teaching that we are guilty because of Adam's sin is called the "doctrine of federal representation" or the "doctrine of original sin." Both doctrines describe the same event from a somewhat different perspective.

These doctrines were so prevalent in the early church and during the Reformation that nobody ever dreamed of questioning them. During the last centuries, these doctrines, so loved by our Christian forefathers, have fallen into disuse and in some cases even reproach. A.W. Pink, a great theologian of the last century, also lamented the absence of modern works on representation by saying, *"I wish someone in our day would write a definitive work on the doctrine of federal representation."*

Though I can't write a treatise on the subject, I will write a sentence that summarizes the doctrine. Read the next sentence carefully because it is the foundation upon which the gospel is built: *God appointed Adam as the representative for the human race in the courtroom of heaven.*

The word *representative* means *"one who acts or stands in the place of."* For instance, in Washington D.C. we have a House of Representatives. Each person in that House *"acts or stands in the place of"* the people he or she represents. The congressman from the

> ❧
> *God appointed Adam as the representative for the human race in the courtroom of heaven.*
> ❧

Sixth District of Oklahoma *"acts or stands in my place"* in Washington D. C. When he votes, I vote. When our representative speaks, we are speaking, because he stands in our place. "Federal representation" speaks of one person representing a designated group of people.

MY FIRST REPRESENTATIVE BEFORE GOD BLEW IT

God made Adam to be our representative before Him in heaven. God gave Adam one prohibition: not to eat of the tree of the knowledge of good and evil. If Adam ate of that tree, he would die.

If Adam had chosen to obey God, he and his posterity (that means us) would have lived forever. Adam disobeyed God so he died, and all his children (you and I included) will die. Our forefather's choice became our choice because he represented us.

Physical death and eternal death are the result of *Adam's* sin. God has every right to condemn us because this "original sin" is passed to us all. David said. *"In sin did my mother conceive me"* (Psalms 51:5).

This is why we teach little Junior to share his toys, not steal. This is why little Suzie must be taught to tell the truth and not lie. We are sinful by nature.

This sinful nature, within all of us, is confirmation of our guilt in Adam. However, sinners are condemned because of *Adam*'s sin; personal sins only aggravate the punishment. The nineteenth century evangelist, Robert Haldane, put it this way: *"Instead of dying for their actual sins, death is to all men the penalty of the first sin."*

THE BIBLICAL BASIS FOR REPRESENTATION

The Apostle Paul went to great pains to show the truth of Adam's representation to the early church in Rome. Paul knew that until sinners understood the depth of their guilt and condemnation in Adam, they would never appreciate the depth of God's grace in Christ.

Paul said, *"Wherefore, as by **one man** [Adam] sin entered into the world, and death by sin; **and so death passed upon all men, for that all have sinned** [emphasis mine]"* (Romans 5:12 KJV).

Due to the tense of the verbs in the original, the meaning is as follows:

All people die because all people sinned in Adam.

The Bible, the early church, the reformers, and great theologians of centuries past have emphatically stated:

It was by one man that men became sinners, hence all men die.

This is very bad news. It is such bad news that it raises the strongest of objections from people who first hear it. But if we object to this bad news that the Bible clearly presents as truth, then we are ultimately objecting to that which will bring hope to our soul—the good news!

Suppose you are a nurse in a cancer hospital and work with many patients undergoing chemotherapy. The doctors tell you the proper dosage of chemotherapy for your patients, and you administer the chemo, going about your business with very little emotion.

Then one day you are told that you have cancer. All of a sudden, all the good news of what chemotherapy can do for cancer patients becomes *very good* news! Why? Because the bad news has become very personal and real to you.

We will never fully understand what it means to be a Christian and in Christ until we first understand what it means to be a sinner and to be in Adam. Death is the result of Adam's sin. We die because we were in Adam when he rebelled against our Creator. Babies die because we were all in Adam when he sinned.

The good news of the gospel is that even though sinners are guilty and condemned by one man's (Adam's) disobedience to God's law, God has determined to *justify many sinners through another man's* (Jesus') *obedience* to God's law.

Pardon Is Good, But Not Enough

God could simply say *"I pardon you,"* to sinners, but that would not set the account straight with Him. He demands perfection; *"Be perfect, even as your Father in heaven is perfect"* (Matthew 5:48). If He simply forgave us, we would still not be righteous, and His justice would be slighted. In short, He wouldn't enjoy our company.

But if somehow God declares us righteous (fully obedient to Him), then we would be justified before Him. The debt we owe God because of sin would be wiped off His books. His blessings would be added to our account because He declares us fully obedient to His law. Jesus Christ makes justification of sinners possible.

Paul put it like this, *"For God has made Christ to be sin for us, who knew no sin; that we might be made the righteousness of God in him"* (II Corinthians 5:21).

If we are to be approved by a holy God, Christ must make us approved. Our faith must be in Him. Our trust must be in His work for us.

The good news is that God embraces all those who embrace His Son. But He is angry with anyone who rejects His Son. *"Kiss the Son, lest he be angry" (Psalm 2:12).*

THE DIFFERENCE BETWEEN PARDON AND JUSTIFICATION

Christians often sing songs of pardon and forgiveness, but when is the last time we sang a hymn on justification? The old-timers used to write most of their hymns on this theme. But many of us simply stop short of an understanding of forgiveness.

Though pardon (forgiveness) and justification have several things in common, justification should be distinguished from the grace of forgiveness in the following ways:

When God forgives me, he removes my punishment; but when God justifies me, he calls me perfectly righteous and holy. In the Bible, the word, *justify* is used in a forensic or legal sense. Its meaning is not *"to make just or righteous,"* but *"to declare judicially that one is in harmony with the law."* Paul uses this word often in the book of Romans. The sinner who has faith in Christ is *declared* by God to be righteous.

The opposite of God's condemnation for sinners is God declaring sinners righteous. *"He is righteous who is judged to be in the right"* (Deuteronomy 25:1). John Gill said:

Sinners . . . according to the doctrine of justification . . . are justified by the obedience and blood of Christ, cleared of all charges, acquitted and absolved, and freed from all condemnation and death and given eternal life.

When God forgives me, He removes my filthy garments of sin; but when He justifies me, He covers me in the spotless coat of Christ's righteousness. A beautiful story from the Old Testament illustrates justification. The prophet Zechariah tells of Joshua standing before the angel of the Lord, with Satan standing at his right hand to accuse or resist him. Put yourself in Joshua's place. One of these days you *will* stand before the throne of God.

> *And the Lord said unto Satan, The Lord rebuke thee, O Satan . . . Is not this a brand plucked out of the fire?* [Did not God pluck *you*, as well, out of the fires of hell?]
> *Now Joshua was clothed with filthy garments, and stood before the angel. And he answered and spake unto those that stood before him, saying, Take away the filthy garments from him. And unto him he said, Behold I have caused thine iniquity to pass from thee, and I will clothe thee with change of raiment.* (Zechariah 3:2-4 KJV)

If we ever come before God clothed in *our* good works, we will be condemned by God. But if we come before God clothed, by faith, in the righteousness of Jesus Christ (Scripture calls this 'the wedding garment'), then we are justified in the eyes of a holy God. There is no hope for any sinner apart from being clothed in the righteousness of Jesus Christ.

When God forgives me, I am not entitled to any of His blessings; but when God covers me with the righteousness of Christ, I am given all the blessings due Christ. An analogy of this is in the Old Testament story of twin brothers, Jacob and Esau. Jacob and Esau were to receive an inheritance. Esau, the firstborn, was to receive the double portion of the blessing from his prosperous father, Isaac. But Jacob, the younger of the twins, clothed himself in the garments of Esau in order to deceive his very old, nearly-blind father. He even put goat skins on his hands and neck so that he would feel and smell like the hairy outdoorsman, Esau. When Isaac reached out to touch Jacob he asked, *"My son Esau?"* Jacob answered, *"I am."* Then Isaac kissed Jacob and blessed him because Jacob was covered in the garments of Esau, the son whom Isaac loved (Genesis 27).

When you and I come before God and His throne of grace, we must come clothed in the goodness of Jesus Christ or dare not approach at all. If we come before God any other way, we shall be condemned. But if we come claiming Christ's righteousness as our own, then the God of all blessings shall bless us because we are in Christ.

The death of Jesus Christ secures my forgiveness, but Christ's obedience and resurrection secures my justification before God. Our righteousness is not our own, but His! Until we realize that God declares us righteous because of Christ's obedience, we will always be attempting to create our own righteousness by our good works.

This was the problem of the Jews. They rejected the Messiah and went after their own righteousness. Paul, a Jew himself, said:

> *My heart's desire and prayer to God for the Israelites is that they may be saved. For I can testify that they are zealous for God, but their zeal is not based on knowledge. They did not know the righteousness that comes from God and sought to establish their own; they did not submit to*

God's righteousness. Christ is the end of the law so that
there may be righteousness for everyone who believes.
(Romans 10:1-4)

We are justified because our representative, Jesus Christ,
was obedient. *"And being found in fashion as a man, he
humbled himself, and became
obedient unto death, even the
death of the cross"*
(Philippians 2:8). His
obedience is perfect and

> ✂
> *We are justified because
> our representative, Jesus Christ,
> was obedient.*
> ✂

complete. Our obedience is inadequate and carries the taint
of sin. We can be zealously religious. But if we think that we
can stand before God in our own righteousness, then we are
in trouble! We can never be justified by our righteousness
and our obedience.

Other religions—Buddhism, Islam, Taoism, Hinduism,
Judaism—have a system whereby they build their own
righteousness. Even Christian denominations sometimes
create man-made systems whereby we build our own righteousness.

Once Mother Teresa was asked, "Do you ever try to make
converts?" She responded, "If by a convert you mean do I try
to convert people to be better Buddhists? Do I try to convert
people to be better Muslims? Yes I do." How sad.

But sometimes we pastors are also guilty of trying to
make others become better Baptists, or Methodists, or
Pentecostals, etc. Trying to make people "better" religious
people will not justify them. Sinners are justified by the One
who obeyed God's law perfectly as their substitute or representative.

ALL A WORK OF GOD

To be justified by God means we are loved, honored, blessed, and treated *just as if* we never sinned and *just as if* we fully obeyed. All of this grace is given to sinners by God through the person and work of the Lord Jesus Christ. He alone pardons a sinner—He alone declares a sinner fully righteous.

Justification is an act of *God's grace*. It is not earned or deserved by our works of righteousness. It is something that God chooses to do. Other religions point to good works. Only Christianity can point to the goodness of Jesus Christ.

> *After that the kindness and love of God our Savior toward man appeared, **not by works of righteousness which we have done,** but according to His mercy He saved us, by the washing of regeneration, and renewing of the Holy Ghost; which He shed on us abundantly through Jesus Christ our Savior; That being justified by His grace we should be made heirs according to the hope of eternal life.* (Titus 3:4-7 KJV)

Justification is consistent with *God's justice*. God doesn't just look at our sin, wink at it, let it go by and take us to heaven. No! That would be *in*justice. That would be as if a judge let a guilty murderer go absolutely free! God doesn't do that.

What does He do? He takes our sin and places it upon Jesus Christ. He punishes the sinless Lord Jesus in our stead, as our substitutionary sacrifice. Only through the imputation of our sin to Christ, and the imputation of His righteousness to us, are we justified in the eyes of God. God remains just in punishing sin, while at the same time being gracious to sinners.

*Being justified freely by His grace through the redemp-
tion that is in Christ Jesus; Whom God has set forth to be
a propitiation through faith in his blood, to declare His
righteousness for the remission of sins that are passed,
through the forbearance of God; to declare, I say, at this
time His righteousness; that He* [that is God] *might be
just, and the justifier of him which believes in Jesus.*
(Romans 3:24-26 KJV)

Justification is *universal*. God has chosen to justify a
multitude of sinners from every tribe, race, and nation of the
entire world. *"And has redeemed us to God by your* [Christ's]
blood out of every kindred, and tongue, and people, and nation"
(Revelation 5:9). This is why we send out missionaries! God
has His people in all the nations.

Justification encompasses *everyone* in the family of Christ.
All the elect, *all* their sins, *all* them that believe. *"Therefore by
the offence of one* [Adam] *judgment came upon all men to
condemnation; even so by the righteousness of one* [Jesus], *the free
gift came upon all men unto justification of life"* (Romans 5:18).
Jesus came to accomplish salvation on behalf of those God
has given Him. These people are known by God from eternity, but are known by us in time as those who come to faith
in Jesus Christ.

Faith is the vehicle through which we receive (become
aware of) our election. But faith in Christ doesn't always look
the same. Some have "great" faith, and some have faith as
small as a "mustard seed."

**Justification is an *eternal* declaration of God, secured
by Christ and received by faith.** Because justification is a
gift of God and because God is eternal and will never fail,
then all of the gifts associated with justification will never fail.
These gifts include the righteousness of Christ and the faith

of Christ that God freely gives to those whom He declares justified in His Son.

This simply means that God loved us before we turned to Him. He sought us before we ever sought Him. His love for His people is from eternity because He chose to love them. His love for sinners compelled Him to send His Son to redeem them (John 3:16).

It is "just-as-if-I" never sinned.

Isn't There Something I Can Do?

There is a common belief that if a person is good from a human perspective, then God has an obligation to receive them into heaven. The late Mr. Rogers, host of the popular children's show, is believed to have been a very good man. If Mr. Rogers did all the good things reported of him, surely God took him to heaven because he was so good. Mother Teresa gave her life to the poor. Since she did so many good works surely God took her to heaven. If Mr. Rogers and Mother Teresa are in heaven, it is because of the work of Christ—not their own good works.

Some years ago several Hollywood actors, athletes, and people who have the respect of the world, gathered to cut an album. This album was to benefit people in Africa suffering from the effects of famine. From a human perspective, what they did was wonderful. They held hands and sang, "We Are the World." It was a beautiful song. I bought one of the albums. What a *good* thing.

However, when we hold that up to the standard of God, it falls short. How many of those celebrities participated in order to be seen? How many of them gave in order to be recognized? How many did it for their reputations, trying to prove they were basically good?

How many times, when I make hospital visits, do I go only for people to compliment the pastor for going to the hospital? How many times do I do marriage counseling for selfish reasons so that people will think good of me? How many times do we all struggle with our nature of intrinsic evil and selfishness?

We are all in that predicament, every one of us. Even when we think that we are doing good (and as I look around at my church I see many good things being done) when we hold that goodness up to the standard of God, it still smacks of sin.

"There is none that does good, no not one" (Romans 3:12c). Good is the essence of God. In fact, His very name *God* is a derivative of a word for good. God is good. He is the standard. Nobody measures up. The best of our goodness is never good enough. Our best efforts do not begin to measure up to God's standard, for our goodness is like a filthy rag (Isaiah 64:6).

REST IN HIM

People get confused. We think if we can just be like Billy Graham, or Larry Jones, or Mother Teresa, then we will deserve God's favor. There is only one way that Billy Graham, Larry Jones, Mother Teresa, you, or I will be received into the presence of God. It is because of the goodness of our Savior.

No one in the past, present, or future shall ever be declared innocent, justified by God, be treated just as if he or she never sinned, unless that person is found in Christ—clothed in His goodness. When we stand before God, it will not be on our own merits but on the merits and the goodness and the righteousness of the Lord Jesus. When I stand before God, I shall not dare to breathe even an ounce of my own goodness. How dare I say to my Creator, "I am good"? For, my friend, I am not! My Lord Jesus Christ—He alone is good. I rest in Him.

To believe that we can be deserving of His mercy and blessing because of our obedience is the most presumptuous form of pride and self-righteousness. That is why Christianity calls *for faith only*. The hardest thing a person will ever do is to renounce self and, by faith, trust Christ. Why is it so difficult? Because every fiber in our body wants to earn the favor of God.

> *The hardest thing we will ever do is to renounce self and, by faith, trust Christ.*

The First Adam/The Last Adam

Although there are many who believe that there are other ways to God, the Bible teaches that sinners either die in Adam and are judged by a righteous God for both Adam's sin and their personal sins, or are saved in Christ who tasted death for His people. There is no other way.

The sentence of condemnation and the gift of salvation are all the work of two people. Our sentence of condemnation is all the work of the first Adam. The gift of salvation for condemned sinners is all the work of the last Adam (Jesus Christ).

GOOD NEWS FOR SINNERS

I don't know about you, but I know what I was apart from God's grace, and I am now very grateful for what I know myself to be by God's grace—I am justified.

Yes, I know myself to be a sinner. I know that I was a condemned sinner before I was even born. All I ever tried to do in life, whether good or bad, simply compounded and aggravated my condemnation. *But God* loved me so much that He gave His Son for me. He died on a bloody cross as the only qualified substitute who could save me from the death sentence incurred by my federal representative Adam.

That's the good news for sinners. That is the gospel. If you are tired of trying to be religious, if you are ready to realize justification, and if you are excited about experiencing in your heart what God has declared from eternity, then come to Christ. You will find true happiness in who you are and you will be able to say, "I am justified."

Religion keeps us on the trail of seeking justification. We are told to present ourselves to God as totally dedicated servants. We are promised blessings from God if we fully obey His will. Religion promises the blessings of God but actually delivers the burdens of hell. Only Christ sets us free from the burden of guilt and condemnation to rightly enjoy the life God created His people to have.

Although we know ourselves to be sinners, we can know, by faith in Christ, that in the eyes of God it is *"just-as-if-I"* never sinned. And when we stand before God clothed in the righteousness of Christ, it is *"just-as-if-I"* always fully obeyed Him. Why? Because God, by His grace, justifies sinners like you and me through the obedience of Jesus Christ, His beloved Son, who is our faithful, loving Representative.

One of the most important, heartwarming, freeing truths of Scripture regarding who I am by the grace of God has just been explained. God is in the business of taking sinners and justifying them by His grace through faith in His Son (Romans 3:24). This is often called simply being "justified by faith" (Romans 5:1).

Thank God for His grace . . .

Thank God for His Son . . .

Thank God for the gift of faith . . .

Thank God I am justified.

*The doctrines of grace
humble a man
without degrading him;
and exalt a man
without inflating him.*

Charles Hodge

Chapter 6
I AM CHOSEN

He hath chosen us in Him before
the foundation of the world.
Ephesians 1:4a (KJV)

If you are the average North American Christian who has grown up under twentieth century Christian teaching, the idea of being chosen by God is not only foreign to your modern ear, it is something that quite possibly scares you to death.

However, take a moment, and just think about it. Don't think about anyone else—your spouse, your children, your neighbor, or friend. Think how it sounds to *you*, "I am chosen."

Think back to your childhood with those playground games where two captains chose teams. How good did it feel to be chosen right off the bat?

There is something special about being chosen for anything. Spiritually, I am chosen by God. When those words ring in my mind, it thrills my heart. A warmth and a comfort come to me.

ORTHODOX TEACHING

Christians prior to the twentieth century would have considered the wonderful doctrine of election and the truth of being chosen by God to be not only orthodox, but essential to true Christianity.

I would like to bring today's Christians back to the old rock-solid truths of the word of God and our forefathers. I do so for a single purpose because I do not believe that you will ever fully rest in the grace of God, deeply rejoice in His love, and totally understand who you are, until you come to grips with the biblical truth that *you are chosen by God.*

I want to clarify what it means to be chosen by God. I hope and pray that your heart will be warmed, you will be encouraged, and you will draw happiness from God's grace. For you to be happy, regardless of your circumstances, involves being happy in who you are by the grace of God.

SCRIPTURE CONCERNING ELECTION

The doctrine of election might still elude you because you have not focused on the subject. I want to show you just a few of the many Scripture passages that reveal this wonderful truth. Then I will draw some fundamental applications from this great doctrine.

Paul writes to the church at Thessalonica. *"But we are bound to give thanks always to God for you, brethren beloved of the Lord, because* **God has from the beginning chosen you to salvation** *through sanctification of the Spirit and belief of the truth"* (II Thessalonians 2:13). In this verse Paul emphatically says to those Christians in Thessalonica, and indirectly to every Christian (including those reading this book), *"God has from the beginning chosen you to salvation."*

Paul wrote a letter to a disciple named Timothy and said, *"Who* [God] *has saved us, and called us with an holy calling, not according to our works, but according to **His own purpose** and grace, which was given us in Christ Jesus before the world began"* (II Timothy 1:9).

Jesus, Himself, said to His disciples, *"You have not chosen Me, but **I have chosen you**, and ordained you, that you should go and bring forth fruit, and that your fruit should remain: that whatsoever you shall ask of the Father in My name, He may give to you"* (John 15:16).

These are just samples of verses found throughout Scripture teaching that God chose us to salvation—that He ordained His people to be forgiven. To deny the doctrine of election is to deny the Scriptures. No Christian can say that election is not taught in Scripture—because it is. We cannot avoid it.

Based upon the truths found in these verses, this is what I mean when I say, "I am chosen": God chose me to salvation before the foundation of the world. In His great love for sinners, He set me apart to take me to heaven. Jesus Christ paid the price for my sins and, in the fullness of time, He gives me the gifts and graces associated with salvation.

Anyone who *has come* to faith in Christ and knows Him in a personal, living relationship as Lord and Savior has been chosen by God; and anyone who *will come* to faith in Jesus Christ has been chosen by God.

THE FOOLISH OF THIS WORLD

Unlike being chosen by someone in the world because we are worthy, God chooses the unworthy! His ways are vastly different from our ways.

> *For ye see your calling, brethren, how that not many*
> *wise men after the flesh, not many mighty, not many noble*
> *are called:* **But God hath chosen the foolish things of the**
> **world** *to confound the wise; and God hath chosen the*
> *weak things of the world to confound the things which are*
> *mighty; and base things of the world, and things which*
> *are despised, hath God chosen, yea, and things which are*
> *not, to bring to nought things that are: That no flesh*
> *should glory in his presence. But of Him are ye in Christ*
> *Jesus, who of God is made unto us wisdom, and righteous-*
> *ness, and sanctification, and redemption: That, according*
> *as it is written, He that glories let him glory in the Lord.*
> (I Corinthians 1:26-31 KJV)

God has chosen the foolish of this world—the base things. He has chosen men, women, boys, and girls who have nothing of which to be proud.

WHAT DOES IT MEAN TO BE CHOSEN?

There are seven great truths on which we can rely concerning God's election of us.

God loves me because God has chosen to love me. God has chosen me out of His love. He loves me because of who He is—the God of love.

Don't distort the doctrine of election. Don't say that God loves us because we have done something for Him. That waters down the Gospel! Don't say that God loves us because we're beautiful in His eyes. There is a beauty in the eyes of God toward us, but it is the beauty of what we will *become* by His grace. By His grace, we will become the bride of Christ, and, by His grace, we will reach heaven, the place where we belong.

Don't think that God looked down through the future and saw what we would promise Him, what we would say, how we would join the church, how we would follow Him, and then said, "Aha! There's a good person, I'll choose her." No, no, no, and a thousand times no!

Can you imagine why God would choose a vile, wretched, godforsaken sinner like you or like me? Can you imagine why God would love us? It is only because He is a God of love. He is in love with sinners.

Because of His great love for you and me, He gave us His Son who died on the cross. Jesus took our place and took upon Himself our sins. In His great love for us, He has taught us what it means to love without conditions.

When we grasp the fact that we are saved, not because we are worthy, not because of anything we have done, not because of any inherent good within us, but because God has chosen to love us; it will cause us to love Him in return. It will also help us to love others with the same kind of unconditional love.

Think about what the Scripture means when it says, "God is love." Look again at Chapter Four of this book for a description of the unconditional love God has for His people. He does not love us because we are worthy of His love or because we meet His standard.

John Blanchard says it like this: "As Christians we ought always to remember that the Lord called us to Himself, not because of our virtues, but in spite of our vices."[1]

> *The Lord called us to Himself, not because of our virtues, but in spite of our vices.*

We have no room to boast before God. Charles Hodge said, "The doctrine of election humbles a man without degrading him; and exalts a man without inflating him."

Do you know the difference between true, biblical Christianity and earthly, man-made religion? True, biblical Christianity presents good news to sinners, and the good news is this: We are all sinners. The only hope we have is for a loving God who, in His love for sinners, sent His Son to pay the price we owe, to die on the cross in our stead, bearing the wrath of our Creator. If any sinner, regardless of race, color, or creed, will bow his or her knee in a total forsaking of self and total trust in God, who gave us His Son, for salvation; that sinner will be saved.

But a self-righteous, religious Pharisee will tell us this: "Nope, what you need to do is to get religion. You need to join our church. We will teach you how to follow God. We will teach you how you can become a better person. Within every man, within every woman, there is this innate goodness. All we need to do is fan the flame, and we will make you better. Come follow our teaching. We will show you how to live by our rules." That is man-made religion!

The only reason we ever fell on our faces and came to the place where we trusted in Jesus Christ alone is because God, in His love for us, softened that old self-righteous, hardened heart and brought us to our knees. God's choosing of us leaves no room for boasting. We cannot say to another, "I am so much better than you—look at me, and how I am. Be like me. God will accept you." We have no room to boast. All we can say to others is, "God loves sinners, like me, and sent His Son to die for the ungodly, like me."

Once God saves me, I am saved forever. We Baptists call this "once saved, always saved." The reason Baptists, Anglicans, many Methodists (like George Whitefield), and other denominations have always believed in eternal security is because, in the past, they understood the biblical doctrine of election. God chose us; therefore, we can never be lost.

The reason many of today's denominations deny eternal security is because they deny election. But, down deep within, there is a desire to know without a doubt that one's salvation is secure. No one wants to go through life questioning his or her security.

We *cannot* believe in eternal security, biblically or logically, unless we believe that God chose us for this reason: If *He* chose us, then *He* keeps us. But if we save ourselves by *our* choice, then what's to prevent us from banning ourselves from God's grace by renouncing our former choice? If we save ourselves—that is, if we just decide, through a rational decision, that being a Christian is a good thing to be; if we just one day decide, "Hey, yeah, I'm going to follow Christ"—then it would be possible that someday we can just decide we are not going to follow Christ.

However, if the Spirit of God changes our hearts, and if God sets His power upon our lives and saves us, then nothing will ever pluck us from Him. The Puritan, Thomas Watson, said, "God never repents of His electing love."

When God sets His love upon us, He sends His Holy Spirit to soften us, to bring us to an acknowledgment of Jesus Christ as our Lord and Savior. When He saves us (for salvation is of the Lord), when He writes our name on the palm of His hand, when He puts us as a jewel upon the breastplate of His heart, when He has us as His child, when He chooses us as His Son's bride, then He will never, ever remove His love from us.

God's love for us remains constant. John Flavel said, "As God did not at first choose you because you were high, so He will not forsake you because you are low." His love does not go up when we are better and down when we are worse. We need never doubt His love.

Man-made religion tells us that God is more in love with us when we become more perfect and insists that God is more pleased with us, will bless us more, will set His love upon us, or be happier with us when we begin to meet a standard.

True Christianity and the old-time Gospel tell us that God is in the business of loving sinners and conforming them to the image of His Son. It is a work that *He* is doing within us. He does it through His church and through the work of His Word. In His providence, He does it through the work of circumstances in our lives. *He* is conforming us to the image of His Son.

> *God never repents of His electing love.*

We may receive the loving discipline of the Lord when we begin to stray from God. But recognize that, in His love, God is drawing us to Himself.

A desire for holiness is the evidence of our election. Maybe you are asking yourself, "How do I know whether or not God has chosen me?" According to Matthew Henry, "None can know their election, but by their conformity to Christ; for all that are chosen are chosen to sanctification."

The evidence of our election is a love for Christ and a desire to be more like Him. Anyone who says, "Hey listen, I'm part of God's elect. I've been chosen by God," but lacks faith in Christ, repentance of sin, or a life that looks more and more like Christ is lying.

Only the softening work of the Holy Spirit will ever produce the kind of life that could be called truly Christian. We can try to get people to obey what God says, but if grace has never inhabited their hearts, it is an impossible task.

Religion has it backwards. It tells us to come to church and commit and recommit to be better, to go after Jesus, to ask, "What would Jesus do in this situation?" All those things are good. But the most important question to ask is: "Am I a child of God?"

As children of God we know that it is an impossible possibility (see Chapter Twelve) to reach God's standard by our own efforts. We know that our holiness is solely based on who we are in Jesus Christ. We are clothed in His righteousness. Any holiness that we have is what He is produc-

> *Do I live before men a holy life? It is not I, but Christ who lives in me.*

ing in us. We can never produce it ourselves! As C. H. Spurgeon says, "Do I live before men a holy life? It is not I, but Christ who lives in me."

If you are concerned about whether or not God has set His electing love upon you, ask yourself these questions: Do you love the Lord Jesus? Does your heart go out to Him? Do you love the things that He says? Do you love the things that He calls you to do? Do you have an affinity for the word of God? Do you want your life to be conformed to the way Christ lived?

It doesn't mean that we will not struggle with sin. It means that where there is grace, there is always repentance of sin. Where there is grace, there is always faith that God forgives. Where there is grace, there is always a growth in holiness. That is the evidence of election.

You might be thinking, "How introspective can you get?" That's a good question because we have to be careful. Sometimes we look so deeply that we see ourselves for who we really are. Then we despair and think there is no holiness, no grace, no faith, no repentance. But when we get to that point of desperation, God is glorified. Because then, through the eyes of faith, we see Christ for who He is and cling to Him. If the Spirit of Christ has done such a marvelous work in our hearts, we fall in love with Him and would rather die than renounce our love for the One who saved us.

Faith and repentance are important. George Whitefield said, "Let a man go to the grammar school of faith and repentance before he goes to the university of election and predestination." If you are struggling with the concepts of election and predestination, don't try to tackle those until you first understand the importance of faith and repentance.

There may be some reading this book who don't know Christ. You may be saying to yourself, "Wade, I'm reading about this doctrine of election. If what you are saying is that if God chooses me, I'll be saved; but if He bypasses me, I won't be saved; then I'll just sit back, and it will be God's fault if I'm not saved."

Let me give you a word of warning and speak directly to your soul. Faith and repentance, though gifts, are your responsibility to possess.

You might say, "But I don't understand. I am without Christ and I need the Lord Jesus, but if I understand you correctly, for me to come to Christ involves His doing a work of grace within my heart. He has not done it!"

Do you want Him to do it? If, with a broken heart you say, "Oh yes, I desperately want God to invade my life, to forgive me of my sins, to turn my life around."

Then I say to you, "The reason you want it is because God, in His sovereign grace and love for you, has driven you to the very place of desiring Christ."

If you say, "I don't want it—and it's God's fault!" I say to you, "It is not God's fault, it is yours!" When you stand before God, shake your fist at Him, and say, "Oh, but if You had only changed my heart I would have been saved," you know what He'll say to you? He will say, "You never wanted it. You never called out to Me, because you were a rebel against Me."

But if you say to Him, "I couldn't call out, because it was not within me!" Then the Lord will say, "Oh, my dear friend, you read a book that showed you that you were a sinner, that Jesus Christ came and died for sinners, and that your only hope was Jesus Christ. But you put that book down and said, 'I refuse to come to Christ!' You are responsible for your sin."

You say, "Wait a minute, that's circular reasoning." No, it is not. If a man winds up in hell, it's his fault. But if a man winds up in heaven, God gets all the credit. I realize that many modern Christians vehemently oppose this kind of preaching. But I plead the word of God and must stand on what He says.

The reason that you don't turn to Christ, that you are in your sin and a rebel against God, is not God's fault—it is yours! You have chosen to go your own way as Adam chose to go his own way. When you stand before the Lord, the Gospel will be a word of condemnation to you. There will be no excuse because you have heard that Jesus Christ is the Savior of sinners, and you have heard that *you are a sinner*. God will hold you responsible.

By faith and repentance, we come into the assurance that we have a part and portion in Jesus Christ. There is nothing sweeter than believing in the Lord Jesus Christ. There is nothing grander than, in repen-

> ❧
> *Go to the grammar school of faith and repentance before the university of election.*
> ❧

tance, following Christ. It is a gift. Christ must do it. It is something that the Holy Spirit produces.

Comfort and rest are a product of understanding the doctrine of election. We will be able to rest in His love all of our lives.

When we come to the place where we can rest in the fact that God in His love chose us and the reason that we love Christ is because He chose us, then no matter the circumstances—whether we're rich or poor, whether we're powerful or nobody in the eyes if the world, whether we're praised or condemned by men—it matters not. The One who really counts has set His love upon us and, therefore, we can be content. We can be happy regardless of our circumstances.

We can rest in His love, rather than wondering about our goodness. There will come times when we really struggle with our goodness. In fact, the more godly we become, the more sinful we feel. But that's all right. Because where do we turn when we feel sinful? We turn to Jesus Christ and rest in the fact that God loves sinners and accepts anyone who comes to the Lord Jesus Christ.

He accepts us because of the work He has done for us and the work He is doing in us. That is why deep, abiding comfort is produced through the doctrine of election.

RACHELLE'S TESTIMONY

My wife, Rachelle, grew up in a Baptist church. She went to church every Sunday and took part in all the activities. But she had never come to an understanding of the doctrine of election—that God had chosen her.

The first time she ever heard the possibility that God had chosen her to salvation, and that God's love for her was due to His choosing to love her, rather than her meeting a standard or performing; she began to doubt her salvation. She began to wonder whether or not God had truly chosen her.

I can remember her talking to me about this. She said, "Wade, I am beginning to see in Scripture how a person is saved because God has chosen to save them, how God sent His Son to die for them, and His Spirit to convert them. But I'm beginning to wonder whether or not that's taken place in my life."

I said, "Sweetheart, let me ask you a question. Do you sense your sin?"

"Oh yes!"

"Do you feel your need of a Savior?"

"Oh yes!"

Then I showed her the promises of God's word, which assure us that whosoever will may come.

I shared an illustration with her that someone had once shared with me: When you come to the door to heaven there is a sign that says, "WHOSOEVER WILL MAY ENTER."

After you go through the door you will see that on the other side the sign says, "YOU HAVE NOT CHOSEN ME—I HAVE CHOSEN YOU."

Rachelle began working through this and began to realize that the doctrine of election should keep no one from coming to Christ. In talking together and reading the Scriptures, she saw the love of Christ for those who embrace the Son. She realized that His choice of her is not due to anything she has done, but due solely to His sovereign and electing love.

Her Christian life literally turned around. When she came to the deep, abiding conviction that God chose her, loves her, saves her, blesses her, embraces her, and will never forsake her because He has chosen to do so; her walk with the Lord was never the same. She has learned to be happy in what she is regardless of her circumstances. She knows that even if everyone else forsakes her, her God will never leave her.

Who can she say she is? Rachelle can say, "I am chosen. I am Rachelle Burleson, chosen of God."

I simply say to you, if you are a sinner, like me and like her—and you are—and you want that kind of relationship with God, surrender your life to God's sovereignty. He alone can save sinners. He alone can turn the life of a sinner around.

The fact that God, in love for sinners like us, has *chosen* to love and redeem us is almost beyond comprehension. B. B. Warfield says, "The marvel of marvels is not that God, in His infinite love, has not elected all of this guilty race to be saved, but that He has elected any."

*Sometimes I think
the church would be better off
if we would call a moratorium
on activity for about six weeks,
and we just waited on God
to see what He is waiting to do for us.*

A.W. Tozer

Chapter 7
I Am Blessed

Blessed be the God and Father of our Lord Jesus Christ,
who hath blessed us with
all spiritual blessings in heavenly places in Christ.
Ephesians 1:3 (KJV)

My wife and I emphatically disagreed with a statement made at a marriage retreat we attended.

The conference leader said it was impossible for a person to be blessed, happy, or content without a spouse. He said that God designed a man to need a woman and designed a woman to need a man.

The reason we emphatically disagree is because we see in Scripture that God has designed the living of life in such a way, that if we come to know Christ, and if we grow in grace and the knowledge of who He is, we can be happy. It makes no difference if we are married, single, divorced, or widowed. We can be content, happy, and joyful in a relationship with God alone. God's blessings are not about circumstances.

This chapter is for those who have been taught that when we follow certain principles or perform to certain expectations of the church—or the minister, or a conference leader, or your view of the standard of Scripture, or even God—then God will bless us. We have grown up in a Christian environment and atmosphere that has been based upon performance. This misguided belief leads to a maladjusted life and burnout.

Even though the belief that we are happy or blessed if we follow certain guidelines is preached from many pulpits, by pastors who firmly believe it to be biblical truth; it is not biblical truth. Let's see what the Bible really has to say about "I am blessed."

THE TRUTH OF SCRIPTURE

Some of the error about what Scripture has to say about blessing is due to confusion between the Old Covenant and the New Covenant. The Old Covenant, found within the Old Testament, was made between God and Israel and is conditional in many aspects. The New Covenant is not. There are glimpses of the New Covenant in the Old Testament, but it is revealed clearly in the New Testament.

When we read the Old Testament, we come across many kinds of promises where God says to Israel, "*If* you do this, *then* I will bless you. *If* you obey Me, *then* I will bless you." We must be careful how we apply these principles because the Old Covenant is a covenant of law that the New Covenant has fulfilled and abolished. That is why every Christian who is a legalist is basing his life on Old Covenant principles.

No one in the Old Covenant could fulfill the Law. But when the Lord Jesus came, every precept, every jot, every tittle, every detail of the Law was fulfilled. He was blessed because He was righteous. When He died on the cross, our sins were imputed to Him. Believers find that His righteousness is imputed to them. We are blessed because of Christ's righteousness, rather than the Old Covenant manner of always obeying the Law. Our blessings are secured in the obedience of Jesus Christ, not in our performance. When we understand Christ and what He accomplished, then we can rest in Him.

Obedience *does* bring blessing. The question is simple: *Whose* obedience? Yours or Christ's?

We can learn two important truths about God's blessing in Paul's letter to the Ephesians. Paul says, *"God the Father has blessed us with all spiritual blessings in heavenly places"* (Ephesians 1:3).

First, He *has* already blessed us. God's blessing of us is *past tense*. This verse does not say, "He *will* bless us"; it says, "He *has* blessed us."

Second, He has blessed us with *all* spiritual blessings. It does not say He has blessed us with *some* spiritual blessings; it says He has blessed us with *all* spiritual blessings.

Why has God blessed us? Later in Ephesians Paul tells us that God has done this so *"that in the ages to come He might show the exceeding riches of His grace in His kindness toward us through Christ Jesus"* (Ephesians 2:7). God has blessed us, by His good pleasure, not because of anything we have done, but because He has determined to bless us in Christ. He has done this in order that He might reveal to His people for eternity all that He has done for them. God delights as we praise Him for what He has done for us.

COMMON MISCONCEPTIONS

Although they know these Scriptural truths about God's blessing, some Christian teachers and preachers say things that sound good on the surface and seem to be right, but are in fact unbiblical.

For example they say, "God helps those who help themselves." I know what they mean when they say that. They have a good intent. We should not just sit back and say, "Well, if it's going to happen, it's going to happen." But the statement, "God helps those who help themselves," is not biblical. In the spiritual realm, which is where we receive forgiveness from God, love from God, mercy from His hand, and pleasure from Him toward us, there is nothing we can do to earn His blessings. To say, "God helps those who help themselves," suggests that we can earn His help, His favor, His benefit. That is not what the Bible teaches.

Well-meaning people also say, "Salvation is God's gift to us—our lives are our gift to God." Again, I know what they mean when they say that. They mean, "God has loved me enough to save me, so I am going to love Him enough to give Him my life." That is a beautiful intention. It really is. I appreciate somebody who desires to give his or her life to the Lord Jesus Christ.

They fail to understand, however, that their life, given to the Lord Jesus Christ in servitude to His lordship, is not something that they just happen to decide to do. It is not something that they just happen to choose. Rather, it was *"God at work in you both to will and to do His good pleasure"* (Philippians 2:13). Our obedience to the Lord is a gift from God given to us. Not only is our salvation a gift from God, so is our very life. Our goodness only comes from God's goodness. If we have any goodness at all, it is because His goodness is implanted within our heart, and we are good from the inside out.

> ❧
> *God's goodness is the root of all goodness. Our goodness springs out of His goodness.*
> ❧

I also hear, "You really must pull yourself up by your own bootstraps." Again, I know what the intent is. You should work, get out of the doldrums, and pull yourself up.

Within every one of these unbiblical sayings is the misconception that if we want to be blessed by God we must do certain things. When Christian leaders teach this, they will usually say that God will bless us if we teach Sunday school, give money to the church, or do things for God and serve and obey Him. We feel guilty if we don't, and hope for blessings if we do.

THE "SNOW WHITE SYNDROME"

Today's churches have communicated to people for so long that God will only bless us if we are a certain way, or behave a certain way, or act a certain way, or do a certain thing, that we develop what I call the "Snow White Syndrome."

Here is what I mean. We constantly hear about God's standard, His expectations, and our responsibility. We come to church and are told what we ought to do, what we should do, what we could do, what we should not do, what we ought not to do—over, and over, and over.

Ingrained within today's Christian is the mistaken notion that we must be "Snow White" in order for God to bless us. Obviously none of us are "Snow White." So what do we do? We hide the dirt. We cannot let anybody see the shortcomings of our lives, so we cover them up. We hide behind our shell. We build a facade.

As kindly and gently as I know how, I want to say that when we do this we become fakes (or sometimes even

"flakes"). We are not real. I am fond of saying that those who
are probably the least genuine on the face of this earth are
professing Christians. (I can say this because I am one.) Why
is this? It is because we hear so often that we should *be* a
certain way to be blessed, that we try to *act* like we are a
certain way or we think we are *not* blessed.

THE WORK ETHIC

Another problem for a Christian today is the heritage of
the Puritan work ethic. I must admit, I am a strong capitalist
and believe that *"if a man will not work he should not eat"*
(II Thessalonians 3:10). I believe we ought to earn our bread
by the sweat of our brow. But, as we are earning our bread
by the sweat of our brow, we need a spirit of humility recognizing that as we work and sweat, it is God who is at work in
us. God gives us the grace to make the money. It is He who
gives the power to work and make wealth.

Even though I strongly believe in the work ethic, I see it
as a problem when it carries over into our relationship with
God. We mistakenly think that God will give to us in proportion to what we give to Him. We think that if we would be a
missionary, or pastor, or get involved in the church, or teach
Sunday school, or do all the good activities we can, then God
will bless us more. Pastors and church leaders must *never*
encourage people to serve God in the church in order to be
more blessed. Even if the church desperately needs Sunday
school teachers, we must not expect people to do anything
the Lord has not called them to do.

Within our churches, we begin to develop seemingly
different levels of Christians depending upon the level of

their performance. For instance, we have (what we consider) the "committed Christian" who is fully involved in the church. Then a little lower down is the Christian who is, perhaps, just a "Sunday benchwarmer." Further down is the Christian who may be considered a "backslider." The implication is that God blesses the Christian who seems to be on a *higher level* more than the one who might be on a *lower level*.

It just is not so. The blessings of God are given to *every* believer *solely* because of the obedience of Jesus Christ.

VALID TEACHING FROM MEN OF GOD

All of these misconceptions continue to be taught by well-meaning Christians, but there are some men of God who have insights more consistent with biblical teaching:

Sir Fred Catherwood: "We are saved, not by our deeds, but by Christ's sacrifice for our misdeeds."

A.W. Tozer: "Sometimes I think the church would be better off if we would call a moratorium on activity for about six weeks, and we just waited on God to see what He is waiting to do for us."

Eric Roberts: "Of what use is it to have many irons in the fire if the fire is going out?"

William Tyndale: "God's goodness is the root of all goodness. Our goodness, if we have any, springs out of His goodness."

WE ARE BLESSED BECAUSE OF CHRIST, THEREFORE–

How does it increase our understanding of God to realize that His blessings are founded upon, given, and secured by

Jesus Christ's obedience and death for us on the cross? It is because there are important, valuable truths about the nature of God—His love, His grace, His care, His mercy, and His pleasure in us—that we cannot understand without knowing the valid teachings about blessings.

God's *love* for us does not increase or decrease. God's blessings are due to the obedience of Christ and to His pleasure in us, simply because He has chosen to take His pleasure in us through Christ. His love for us does not increase or decrease in proportion to our love for him.

If all of us were honest, we would say that we have very difficult days when God feels a million miles away—when, for no explanation at all, depression sets upon us like a cloud. Sometimes when people reject us, or when we go through a bad experience, we might feel that God is gone. We might become a little bitter, a little angry. All of us have been there. But if we realize that God's blessings are given through Christ Jesus, then we can understand that His love for us does not decrease when our feelings of love for Him decrease. He loves us unconditionally.

His *grace* to us is given unconditionally. We do not earn more grace by putting out more effort. He blesses us with His grace just because He has chosen to give it to us through Christ Jesus, who made it possible for a Holy God to favor sinners without violating His justice.

If our concept of God's grace is tied to our own performance, then we have no understanding of grace. We have an understanding of the law—but not of grace.

His *care* for us is promised without conditions. He loves us because He is the One who has chosen us, who has drawn us, and who has given us the new birth. We are His children because of *His* work. As His children, He will care for us without conditions.

The idea that God will only care for us when we walk along a certain path, and that He will not care for us if we stray or wander from it, is false. It is true, however, that sin is destructive in its nature. But it is not God who is destroying—it is the

> ✣
> *We are saved, not by our deeds,*
> *but by Christ's sacrifice*
> *for our misdeeds.*
> ✣

sin itself. Even when we wander from the path, He is merciful in withholding the full effects of sin because He loves us and takes pleasure in us.

Just as the shepherd went after the lost sheep and did everything necessary to bring the sheep back, so will God go after His child regardless of the state the child is in. God is not angry with us. His love and pleasure abide with us because of Christ.

His *mercy* for us is sweet and sure every day. If we misunderstand the nature of God's blessings, we will wake up in the morning worried about whether or not God is going to be pleased with us and accept us. We will worry about whether or not we are going to be able to do enough for God each day in order for Him to do enough for us.

Or, we can wake up with a song in our heart because we know that His mercies are new every morning. We can say this is a new day of grace. His mercy for us is so sweet and so sure. We can rest in the mercy of God.

His *pleasure* in us causes Him to never give up on us. Just as the father waited for the prodigal son and allowed the sin of the prodigal son to bring the young man to his senses (Luke 15:11-32), so will God in His providence sometimes allow our sin to break us. If God has chosen to grace us, even our sin, and the discipline associated with it, will be used by God as an ultimate blessing. His blessing is not dependent upon our performance. If we are wounded as a result of succumbing to the enemy's attacks, He will not abandon us. He will take even our failures and bless us through them.

Have you ever been caught up in a particular sin of spirit, word, or deed? You cannot shake it, yet your heart is broken. If your heart is broken when there is sin, that is evidence you are a believer. I have met plenty of lost people who lap up their sin like a dog laps up its vomit, but I have never met a Christian who, when involved in sin, loves his sin. He repents, goes before the Lord, and says to Him, "O Father, I am broken over my sin. Lord, this is wrong. Father, give me the grace, please, to overcome it."

Maybe the next day he struggles with the same sin and begins to feel guilty and to wonder, "How many times can I come to the Lord and ask Him for forgiveness, or confess to Him that I am wrong? How many times can I do that before He gets angry, before He begins to withdraw, before He says, 'I'm tired of you. I give up on you.' "

No matter how difficult our struggles may be, God does not remove His hand of blessing. He will *never* cease to bless us. He will never give up on us because His pleasure in us is due to Christ in us, not to our performance.

HOW THIS AFFECTS OUR RELATIONSHIPS

If we cling to our faulty understanding of blessings, we will have a faulty understanding of the nature of God. Our warped understanding of the nature of God will affect our relationships because the way we treat others is the way we believe God treats us.

If we are critical of others, this means we believe God is critical of us. We don't understand God's unconditional love. Show me a person who can do nothing but criticize by saying, "Why can't you do that better? If you would only do this we'd be happy. Why don't you do what I say? When are you going to listen to me?"—always you, you, you, you— and I will show you a person with a warped relationship with God. They believe God is critical of them, so they become critical of others. They don't see God's unconditional love for them, so they are not able to have unconditional love for others.

If we withhold friendship, it usually means we believe God withholds His friendship from us. If we ever can grasp that God's love, His friendship, His kindness, and His mercy are independent of what we do in our relationship to Him, then it will free us to be kind, loving, merciful, and gracious to those who have wronged us. When we are wronged, offended, and hurt, we will think, "Wait a minute. Even though someone has wronged me, how many times have I wronged God? But He has blessed me, and I am accepted in Christ. So you know what? If God accepts me like that, then I'm going to accept whoever hurts me."

Those who have hatred and bitterness in their hearts are usually those who have no idea what grace is all about. They will sing about it and talk about it, but grace to them is only a word. They have never come to understand it in their hearts.

Our present maladjustment in life is often a result of a warped relationship with God. Pride causes us to refuse to consider that our present difficulties—in marital relationships, in friendships, in our church relationships—our criticism, our withdrawal, all the things that are going on to cause strained relationships, may be, in reality, a reflection of a warped relationship with God.

A barometer of our fellowship and relationship with God is our fellowship and relationship with other Christians. Are we angry? Are we bitter? Do we harbor resentment? Do we shut people off when they offend us?

If there is maladjustment in your life, evaluate why you do what you do for God. Could it be that you really do not understand His love for you? You may think you have to earn His love and blessing.

We will burn out if we think God loves us and blesses us according to our service. If we find ourselves looking around at what others are doing and comparing their service to ours, then we may be on the edge of burnout. We might feel guilty and try to do more, or we might judge

> *Of what use is it to have many irons in the fire if the fire is going out?*

others by their performance. We might say of others, "Why don't they serve God like me? Why don't they teach Sunday school like me? They're not dedicated Christians. They must not love Christ as much as I love Him."

FREE TO SERVE

Why do you do what you do for God? Is it because you think He will love you more, bless you more, or take more pleasure in you the more you do? Do you ever think that

God is closer to you when you are at service for Him, that He draws nearer because of what you do?

If so, then you have a warped understanding of God. You have not realized that He loves you just because He loves you. He blesses you because He has chosen to bless you in Christ Jesus. Your conduct, your good deeds, your works, sure, they are going to be there; but they are not reasons why God blesses you. What we do in service to God ought to be done out of a heart of gratitude for what God *has already done for us!*

When you come to understand this, you will no longer be concerned with how many people know what you do for God. You will no longer be concerned with how often you are complimented for your service to the Lord Jesus. You will no longer look around and see who is noticing what you are doing. It does not make any difference because you already have God's approval, His pleasure, His forgiveness, and His love. You do not need to get your strokes from anybody else.

A full understanding of the nature of God's blessings will free you up in your relationships, and will free you up to serve your Lord in gratitude, joy, and peace.

Stop trusting in yourself. As a believer you *are* blessed. You are blessed by God, independent of who you are and what you do. You can be content no matter your station in life. You can be happy and full of joy whether you are married, divorced, widowed, single, with children, without children, poor, rich, bound, free, master, slave.

You can get up each morning with a song in your heart because you know you have unlocked the secret of being content with who you are. You can say, "By the grace of God I am what I am. I am blessed."

*The further we get from freedom,
the further we get from New Testament
Christianity and the more our religion
resembles every other religion—
merely a system for keeping the basic
instincts of human nature in check.*

Steve Brown

Chapter 8
I AM FREE

Stand fast therefore in the liberty
wherewith Christ hath made us free.
Galatians 5:1a (KJV)

Catch Me if You Can is the story of the life of Frank
Abagnale Jr. In the Steven Spielberg movie, Tom Hanks is
cast as the FBI agent who is pursuing Abagnale, played by
Leonardo DeCaprio. When he was sixteen, Abagnale ran
away from home and began a life of crime. He pretended to
be a doctor, an attorney, and a pilot. He forged checks and
stole over two million dollars from Pan Am Airlines. That
was a lot of money back in the sixties.

The FBI pursued Frank Abagnale Jr. for several years. It
was one of their largest investigations. They finally caught
him in France around his twentieth birthday, extradited him
to the United States, and sentenced him to prison. He had
been in prison for about a year and a half when the FBI
released him on the condition that he work for them to
uncover fraud through check writing and check kiting across
the United States.

In a scene near the end of the movie, Abagnale sees a
pilot's uniform, buys it, and makes his way to the airport.
You just know that he's going back to a life of crime by
pretending to be a pilot. Your heart begins to sink.

As he is walking down the concourse, he hears his name called out. Tom Hanks, the FBI agent, has followed him to the airport. As Abagnale turns around, his pursuer asks him, "Are you leaving?"

Frank says, "Yes I am. I'm just pulled to do what I do."

The agent says, "Okay."

Abagnale, "Aren't you going to stop me?"

The agent replies, "No."

Abagnale, "Why not?"

The agent explains, "Look around. No one is chasing you. You'll be back."

The movie ends with the criminal coming back to the FBI and leaving his criminal ways because nobody is chasing him.

A CHRISTIAN, ABOVE ALL OTHERS, SHOULD BE FREE

The way we stay committed to Christ is by realizing that nobody is chasing us. The law is not on our heels. We are not going to be condemned for our actions.

In this chapter, I want to help you come to the full measure of freedom. What I am saying will probably affect every single person reading this book. It is something that you may have never really considered before.

I want you to see that our freedom is based upon an understanding of, and faith in, what God did for us through Jesus Christ. As believers, we are free. Free from the fear of death, free from the condemnation of sin, free from fear of Satan, free from the bondage of the law, free to live and enjoy life in Christ.

The truth of what Scripture says about our freedom in Christ is so unbelievable that most Christians dismiss it as being impossible. I want to show you that not only is it possible, but it is a reality in your life. If you see what Scripture says and come to some understanding of what I'm attempting to teach in this book, the freedom that you will enjoy will literally lift your soul to the heavens. It will encourage you, inspire you, and set you free.

Jesus himself said, *"I am the way, the truth, and the life"* (John 14:6). If we know Him – the truth – *"the truth will make you free"* (John 8:32). He went on to say, *"If the Son shall make you free, you shall be free indeed"* (John 8: 36).

Paul wrote to the Galatians (who were struggling with the concept of freedom), *"Stand fast therefore in the liberty where Christ has made us free, and do not be entangled again with the yoke of bondage"* (Galatians 5:1).

The Christian life should be measured by freedom. Unfortunately, in my experience, those who seem to lack freedom are sometimes the very ones who are regular in church and profess their Christian faith boldly. I don't understand how they can profess to know the truth that makes them free and yet not be free.

FREEDOM OR BONDAGE

The opposite of freedom is bondage. Many Christians feel themselves to be in bondage to four particular things in their lives.

Many believers feel in bondage to sin. Some, because of this bondage to sin, or at least the thinking that they are in bondage to sin, make excuses, rationalizations, and justifications for their sins.

Some believers who struggle with specific sins try to justify or to feel better about them by blaming their parents, their background, or particular traumas as the reason why they struggle with certain sins. As believers, when we sin, we cannot blame anyone else. We alone are responsible for our sins.

Why is this important? Because once we quit making excuses and call sin what it is, "SIN"—not a weakness, not an illness, not a result of poor parenting, then we can bring it before the only One who can cleanse us of all our iniquities.

Believers need to understand that God has done a wonderful work within our hearts. He has given us the power and the ability to say no to sin. *"For we know that our old self was crucified with Him, so that the body of sin might be rendered powerless, that we should no longer be slaves to sin, because anyone who has died has been freed from sin"* (Romans 6:6, 7).

I am not saying that believers do not sin. We are sometimes capable of the vilest and grossest sins. Nor am I saying that it is possible for us to be completely free from sin—not at all. I am saying that God will not think less of us if there is a compulsion that seems impossible to break, and He will not love us any less if we seem to be stuck in a particular sin.

In Christ, sin has been rendered powerless. We are no longer slaves to sin like those who are lost and without grace. Therefore, when we sin, *which we will*, we must take responsibility for that sin.

If we get in bondage to a particular habit, compulsion, or obsession, be assured that there is power through Christ to break that compulsion. What is required to break sin is to be *honest* about it! The reason we can't be honest about our sin is because we've created an environment where God's people have to pretend that they are without sin. Only grace can give us the ability to *freely* confess and *freely* repent of sin. Sometimes we might need help from others—an accountability group, counseling, or therapy—to break the chains of a particular sin. But we have the responsibility to see sin for what it is, bring it before Him, and let Him guide us.

Peter wrote in his epistle, *"Live as free men; but do not use your freedom as a cover up for evil. Live as servants of God"* (I Peter 2:16).

Some Christians feel in bondage to Satan. They feel that Satan has control over their lives because they have fallen into the old heretical trap called *dualism*, which is the belief that God and Satan are struggling for control of the soul. If Satan has the upper hand, it is going to be a bad day. If God gets the upper hand, it is going to be a good day. They think God and Satan are battling each other for control of their hearts, their desires, and their wills. That is not true at all.

The truth is all people are, by nature, in bondage to Satan. But God sets His people free. *"He* [the Lord] *has rescued us from the dominion of darkness and brought us into the kingdom of the Son He loves"* (Colossians 1:13). We are not the servants of Satan when we are in Christ. We are not in bondage to him. There is no such thing.

Believers are in the camp of grace. We have been rescued from the dominion of the devil. We belong to the Lord Jesus. We are His. He has set us free from our former bondage to Satan and to sin.

Christians in bondage to the law have the false belief that God's blessings, His love, His goodness, His grace, His affection, all of this, is given to a believer because of one's obedience to the law.

Christians in bondage to the law structure a system for themselves. They devise a set of scruples, codes, and high principles. They write their own Christian rule book, and then put themselves in bondage to do everything in their

We are blessed by Christ, not by works.

book down to the last letter. If they perform up to their self-imposed standards, and God doesn't bless them with health, money, etc., they get angry and bitter. Or, if they think they have been blessed by God because they've crossed every *t* and dotted every *i* in their code book, then they get proud of themselves and critical of others.

That is bondage to the law. But Scripture says we are free. Our blessings have come not because of *our* obedience to the law, but rather because of *Christ's* obedience to the law. Our blessings from God come through Christ by faith. *"For Christ is the end of the Law for righteousness, to everyone who believes"* (Romans 10:4).

We will not be blessed by God one iota more because of the law, and our obedience to it, than when we disobey the law because God's blessings are given to us through our faith in Christ.

Let me give an example. Some struggle with what can or should be done on what they would call the Sabbath day. Can a person work on Sunday? Can a person go out to eat on the "Sabbath"? They develop a theology which says: if I *do* certain things on Sunday and *abstain* from other things on Sunday, then God will bless me; but if I *don't do* what God wants me to do on Sunday, and I do things that He doesn't desire for me to do on Sunday, God will not bless me.

As a result, there is conflict as to what can be done to please God in order to be blessed and a tremendous bondage to whatever system they set up for observation of the Sabbath. Paul says, *"Let no man therefore, judge you in meat, or in drink, or in respect of an holy day, or of the new moon, or of the sabbath days; which are a shadow of the things to come; but the body is of Christ"* (Colossians 2:16, 17 KJV).

The premise of one of our conservative Christian movements (which has thousands of followers) is that if you behave a certain way and follow a certain code, whether it be diet, particular ways of educating children, or certain standards for living, then God will bless you. If you don't abide by all of their principles and precepts, you will miss out on the blessing of God. That, I believe, is contrary to the word of God.

The blessings of God are *not* given to us through subjection to the law. The blessings of God are given to us by grace through Jesus Christ. Christ is the end of the law.

Some believers are in bondage to guilt—the guilt that just comes from daily living. Because of grace (for only grace enables us to see ourselves for who we are), we know ourselves to be capable of the vilest sins of heart and life. As a result, we often feel guilty before God.

The more we understand the grace of God, the more guilty we see ourselves to be. And the more we begin to understand the unconditional love of God, the more unworthy of His love we feel. In other words, the closer we come to Christ and the more we know of Him, the worse we will feel about ourselves. We don't *become* worse (as far as sinful actions), but we *feel* worse. Because of grace, we feel our hearts are full of sin. Even the apostle Paul felt himself to be "the chief of sinners" (I Timothy 1:15).

However, Christ came to set us free from the bondage of guilt. The more we grow in grace, the freer we become. But if we don't learn who we are, by the grace of God, we often find ourselves in bondage to guilt. When we are in bondage to the guilt of sin, we do two things:

We try to cover up sin and hide it. We don't want anyone to get close to us because we are afraid of what that other person is going to think of us. We are guilt-ridden and become phonies and hypocrites.

Or, we just give up because we are burned out. We say, "I don't know what to do. I don't know where to turn." We turn our backs on what we know is right because we think we just can't measure up. We run from God because we believe we have to be perfect in order to be loved by God, and we give up trying because we are burned out of trying to measure up and not succeeding.

GOD SEES NO SIN IN HIS PEOPLE

However, as Christians, we can be free from bondage to the guilt of sin. We can be free from the bondage of guilt when we understand that God sees no sin in His people. The eighteenth-century Baptist Dr. John Gill systemized this profound statement in his article "God Sees No Sin in His People." As was the eighteenth century theologian's style, Gill explains three different things he does *not* mean when he says "God sees no sin in His people," and in the fourth statement (the final paragraph) he explains what "God sees no sin in His people" means. Read carefully:

> FIRST, When it is asserted that God sees no sin in His people, the meaning is not that there is not sin in believers, nor any committed by them, or that their sins are no sins, or that their sanctification is perfect in this life.
>
> 1. Sin is in the best of saints; to say otherwise is contrary to Scripture. . . , 'If we say we have no sin we deceive ourselves and the truth is not in us,' I John 1:8.
>
> 2. Sin is not only in the best of saints, but is also committed by them: *"There is not a just man upon earth that doeth good and sinneth not,"* Romans 7:17, 20.
>
> 3. The sins of believers are sins, as well as the sins of others; they are of the same kind and are equally transgressions of the Law, as others are: murder and adultery, committed by David, were sins in him, as well as they are as committed by others; yea, oftentimes the sins of believers are attended with more aggravating circumstances than the sins of other men, being acted against light and knowledge, love, grace and mercy. . . .
>
> 4. The work of sanctification is imperfect in this life; it is a good work begun, but not finished . . . [It will not be until we get to heaven.]
>
> SECONDLY, God's seeing no sin in His people does not impeach His omniscience:. . . *"His eyes are upon the ways of man and He seeth all his goings. There is no darkness nor shadow of death where the workers of iniquity may hide themselves,"* Job 34:21, 22.
>
> THIRDLY, Nor is the meaning of this proposition, that 'God sees no sin in His people,' that He takes no notice of them, nor resents them, nor chastises them in a fatherly way. . . God does not, indeed, punish His people for their sins in a way of *vindictive* wrath and justice; for this is contrary to His justice, and must overthrow the satisfaction of Christ; for either Christ has perfectly satisfied for the sins of His people, or He has not; if He has not, they must satisfy for them themselves; if He has, it is contrary to the justice of God to punish for sin twice, or to require satisfaction, both of the surety [Jesus Christ] and the sinner [you]: but though God does not punish His people for their sins, yet He *chastises* them in a fatherly way.

FOURTHLY, Though God sees sin in His people, as being but in part sanctified, yet He sees no sin in them, as they are perfectly justified; though He sees sin in them with His eye of omniscience, yet not with His eye of revenging justice; though He sees them in respect of His providence, which reaches all things, yet not in respect of justification; though He takes notice of His people's sins so as to chastise them in a *fatherly* way for their good; yet He does not see them, take notice of them, and observe them in a judicial way, so as to impute them to them, or require satisfaction for them. *"Who shall lay anything to the charge of God's elect? It is God that justifieth. Who is he that condemneth? It is Christ that died,"* Romans 8:33, 34. God will not require satisfaction at the hands of His people for their sins; He will not punish them on the account of them; they shall never enter into condemnation *"for there is no condemnation to them that are in Christ Jesus; who walk not after the flesh, but after the Spirit,"* (Romans 8:1).

Do you understand what Dr. Gill is saying? If we could ever grasp this truth, it would set us free. He is saying that God does not punish us for our sins. He punished Christ in our place.

God Does Not Punish Us for Our Sins

You might say, "I don't understand that. I thought God was always punishing me when I fail Him or disobey Him. I always thought God was vindictive and must have satisfaction from me in some way. When I fail Him, I thought I had to make promises in order to make Him feel better about me. If I would just promise to do better in the future, then He would bless me."

No wonder you are in bondage and feel so guilty. You have imposed all these laws and codes of conduct that you live by, and when you see that you don't measure up, you think that God will punish you.

On the other hand, if you think you are measuring up and believe you are meeting your standard, then you become full of pride in your pristine performance. In Chapter Seven, I called this the "Snow White Syndrome." We feel we must be "snow white" in order to be blessed. We may be trying to act "snow white" on the outside, but we have failed to deal with our corrupt hearts.

True Christianity will convince us that we are inherently sinful, then it will point us to a Savior who saves sinners. Mere religion, on the other hand, will try to convince us that we can be good and will drive us to try to do the best we can.

God is holy. He does have a standard. By nature we are in bondage to the Law, in bondage to works, in bondage to a code. We will never be able to meet all the rules and regulations which are imposed upon us. But Christ has met all the rules, in our stead. He died on the cross as a perfectly holy Savior. All of our shortcomings, sins, and failures were placed upon Him who knew no sin—on Him who took the punishment for our sins. Christ came to set His people free.

Through Christ we are blessed, so that even though *"I live, it is no longer really I, but it is Christ in me"* (Galatians 2:20). All the blessings we have received from heaven—all spiritual blessings—are not given to us because of what we have done, promised to do, or will do. All spiritual blessings are given to us because of what Christ has done for His people. We are blessed by *Christ*, not by *works*.

WHAT ABOUT THE LAW?

Soon after I preached a sermon on freedom, a delightful lady came to me and said, "Pastor, I just can't handle this. This is too much for me."

I asked her, "What do you mean?"

She said, "Laws are good. Rules and regulations are wonderful. We have to live by them. If we don't, there are consequences. I can't handle this idea, that there are no laws for the believer!"

I replied, "You misunderstand, I have rules and regulations in my life. I also live by laws."

"But I thought I heard you say that the law was of no effect for the Christian!" she objected.

"Wait—what I said was, 'there's not one condemnation for violations of the law. I could violate every rule and regulation of law in my life every day of my life, and there is not one condemnation from God!'"

She said, "Oh, but there is condemnation from family, from friends, and from government."

I told her, "That is a consequence of one's actions. There are always consequences to one's sin. Nobody would ever say anything differently. But there is not one condemnation from God."

She replied, "I just don't know—that's so scary."

FEAR OF BACKSLIDING

Why is it so scary for us to be free from the bondage of law, and sin, and death, and condemnation?

Steve Brown, writing about Christian freedom, says, "People are living in a prison and have been given the key to their cell door, yet they hide the key and pretend that nothing can be done." He gives some reasons why he believes people are scared to be free. He says they feel secure in their cell, think they deserve to stay there, are afraid of risk, and don't want to lose control.[1]

I would say that some stay in their cells because they are comfortable with the idea that God is going to whack His kids when they cross the line. They believe that the law is what keeps them in check.

Parents say, "Preacher, tell our kids there is law; and if they don't obey the law–whop!–they're gonna get it. Preacher, that's what's gonna keep our kids in line." You might say, "Pastor, the only thing that keeps me in the straight and narrow is this feeling that I'm going to get whacked if I stray! The only reason I am faithful to my wife is fear that God will get me."

No, my friend, that is the only thing that keeps you hiding. That's the thing that keeps you running.

When we understand that the righteousness God demands has been met by Jesus Christ, fulfilled in us, and that we are free from the bondage of sin and death, then no pastor, evangelist, church, or counselor has to tell us to love our husbands or wives. We

> *When you understand freedom, you will be holier than you have ever been.*

don't have to be forced to. The love of Christ for us compels us internally to be faithful to our mates.

So What Are You Afraid Of?

Seriously, what are you afraid of? Are you afraid of the loss of God's love? Read Chapter Four again. Are you afraid that you would go out and do something that you would regret?

Go ahead and be free. You know what you will discover? You will discover that when you understand freedom, you will be holier than you have ever been. But your whole motivation will be different.

When we understand freedom we, as believers, will be more committed, more holy, more loving, more kind, more serving, more prayerful, than we ever dreamed of being under the law. Nobody will need to tell us to worship or make us go to church. The preacher won't have to heap guilt upon us to get us to give. We will give, and we will worship because that will be our hearts' desire.

We will be free to love our spouses and to love them the way they are. We will be free to love and accept our children. We must get out of the captivity of *I have to* and into the liberty of *I am free to*.

Are you free from the bondage of seeking God's favor by your performance? Are you free to live life the way it was intended?

You say, "Pastor, but now wait a minute. You tell that to some people, and they'll go out and live like the devil."

Maybe so. But if they do, and never have any signs of repentance, then it is doubtful that they have ever been touched by the Spirit of God. The freedom we are talking about is found in Christ and can only be experienced by those who embrace Him.

"The law of the spirit of life in Christ Jesus has made me free from the law of sin and death. For what the law could not do, God did" (Romans 8:2, 3).

WHAT DID GOD DO?

The law will never give us freedom because the law is powerless to do that, but God did. We can measure our freedom as a Christian by how much we understand what God did for us through Christ at Calvary.

Let us examine what happened at Calvary: Jesus Christ was the perfect man who lived his life in our stead, as our substitute. All of our sins were placed upon Him. There is no condemnation against us who are in Christ. Therefore, the law of life in Christ has set us free—free from the law of sin and death.

God sees no sin in His people.

We will never understand what it means to live free, to be led by the Spirit, to love people, to free other people up, and to just love life and enjoy God until we understand that nobody is chasing us. The running and hiding is over. God did for us what the law could not do.

When we comprehend what Christ has done for us, we will be like Frank Abagnale Jr. who was set free by the FBI, but then freely came back to work for them.

We will do what we do for Christ because we want to, not because we have to. Everything we do will come from a heart of gratitude, rather than a heart of duty and drudgery.

WHOM DO YOU TRUST?

Suppose we are neighbors, and you call me one day and say, "Wade, my porch is about to cave in. It's really in bad shape. There's a hole in it and I'm afraid to let my kids walk on it. I've had to block it off. Can you help me?"

Then let us suppose that I bring some tools that I had been given for Christmas: a router and a buzz saw (this is obviously not true—it is fantasy) and come over to your house with these new tools and tell you, "Why don't you just go on to work and trust me to repair your porch."

So I get busy. All day I work on your porch. When you come home, to your dismay, you find your porch in worse shape than before. You look at me, and you look at your porch, and you ask, "Wade, what did you do?"

I reply, "Well, I just don't know how to use these tools correctly. I thought I could get the job done. I know that I promised you I'd fix it while you were at work. I'm really sorry."

You say to me, "But what am I to do now?"

I think it over and respond, "Well, you know, hmmm . . . I'll tell you, we have several carpenters in our church. Why don't you call Bill Bickerstaff? He's a master carpenter, and I'm sure he can come help."

The next day Bill comes over and you go off to work. He pours a strong concrete foundation, supports your porch with steel beams, and puts down new wood. When you come home from work, you find that you have a brand new, strong, beautiful porch. What Wade could not do because he is inherently inept at carpentry, Bill did because he is a master carpenter.

Now that a master carpenter has done the restoration, how much freedom would you have with your porch? I think it is directly proportional to how much you trust the master carpenter and understand what he did for you.

Let's say he shows you the concrete foundation, the steel beams, and the new wood. He explains all that he has done and says, "This is the strongest porch that you've ever had."

Then you have confidence to be free to go up and down and do as you please on your porch. You are free to jump on that porch, to call your kids out, sit them down and read stories to them on that porch. You are free to do as you please on the porch because you understand what the master carpenter did to fix the porch.

So it is with the Christian life. We will only be free and confident to live the way we were intended when we understand what God has done for us.

As long as we try to "do-it-ourselves" with God, we will be in bondage to our own futile efforts. When we turn the restoration over to the Master Carpenter, we can trust His perfect workmanship rather than our own defective workmanship.

In Christ we are free. We are free from bondage to sin, bondage to Satan, bondage to the law, and bondage to guilt. God's grace has set us free. Let us learn each day to revel in that freedom.

Plagues and deaths
Around me fly,
Til He bids I cannot die.
Not a single shaft can hit
Til the God of love sees fit.

John Ryland

Chapter 9
I Am Protected

For God hath not given us the spirit of fear;
but of power, and of love, and of a sound mind.
II Timothy 1:7 (KJV)

Several years ago, I met a woman with the most severe anxiety I have ever seen. At her husband's request, I went to their home to visit with her. All she ever did was rock back and forth in her chair.

After many, many minutes of just sitting there trying to get her attention, we finally were able to understand that she was terribly afraid the world was coming to an end. She put herself into such a state of fear that she could do nothing and desired to do nothing—except rock back and forth

Fear is a feeling of anxiety, worry, concern, or terror. Because fear is an emotion, it is difficult to define on an intellectual level. When we use the word *fear,* everyone knows what we are talking about because everyone has experienced it. Fear is very personal and will affect different individuals in different ways. Just as the lady I visited, some are unable to function normally because of fear.

Fear makes us feel vulnerable as if something bad is going to happen to us. We feel we are going to suffer or be under attack. Fear is a result of our belief that we are not protected.

What the Bible Says About Our Protection

This chapter is about what it means for us, as believers, to be protected by the Lord. Several Scripture passages give encouragement when we are feeling fearful.

"Be strong and of a good courage; be not afraid, neither be dismayed; for the Lord your God is with you whereever you go" (Joshua 1:9).

"Be not afraid or dismayed . . . for the battle is not yours, but God's" (II Chronicles 20:15).

"For God has not given us the spirit of fear; but of power, and of love, and of a sound mind" (II Timothy 1:7).

"I will never leave you, nor forsake you" (Hebrews 13:5b).

Two Kinds of Fear

According to Scripture there are two kinds of fear. Godly fear, which is good and is commanded, and ungodly fear, which is not commendable or good and is prohibited.

Godly fear: The writer of Hebrews mentions godly fear: *"Whereby we may serve God acceptably with reverence and godly fear"* (Hebrews 12:28 KJV). To fear God is to have "a reverential affection for God flowing from a sense of His love." It is being in awe of the person of God, recognizing who He is; and because of His power, His authority, His sovereignty, and His providence, having a sense of reverence in His presence. *"The beginning of all wisdom is found in fearing God"* (Proverbs 1:7).

Godly fear is somewhat like the fear we would feel if we ever entered the Oval Office to be introduced to the President of the United States. He is only a human being. But as we walk into his presence, we would find that our heart would beat a little faster, and our knees would grow a little weaker because we are in the presence of power.

So it is with God. He is our Father. We are to be intimate with Him, love Him, and feel affection for Him. But we can never get away from the fact that He is Almighty God. Godly fear is a reverential affection for God flowing from a sense of love.

Ungodly fear: Paul refers to ungodly fear in his letter to Timothy. He tells young Timothy that *"God has not given us the spirit of fear"* (II Timothy 1:7a).

Paul also referred to ungodly fear when he debated the philosophers on Mars Hill in ancient Athens. This was a place where people congregated to debate philosophical and religious issues. Once when Paul was brought there he said, *"Ye men of Athens, I perceive that in all things ye are too superstitious"* (Acts 17:22b KJV). The King James word translated *superstitious* is the Greek word *desidemonia*. This word literally means "fear of demons."

What did Paul mean? He was saying to these philosophers, who loved to debate religious things, "I perceive that you have fear, and it is the fear of demons. You don't reverence God—you tremble at His power as an enemy soldier trembles before the king's court. You are superstitious, and in your superstition you worship all kinds of gods, idols and statues. Lest you think that you have left out some god and he will be offended, you have created one statue inscribed:

'TO THE UNKNOWN GOD' (Acts 17: 23). I perceive you have fear of demons." This superstitious kind of fear that Paul found in Athens is the kind of fear that demons have for God. That is the kind of fear that we are not to have.

Demons obviously are without grace. Jesus Christ said of those who are lost that *"You are of your father the devil"* (John 8:44). So the kind of fear that demons have is the kind of fear that those without grace have.

The superstitious fear of God is natural to every human being. Only the grace of God will free us from *desidemonia,* the ungodly "fear of demons," and teach us a godly fear. *"But by the grace of God I am what I am"* (I Corinthians 15:10).

FIVE FEARS OF THOSE WITHOUT GRACE

Rejection, both by God and man, is a fear of those without grace, and possibly some who are graced by God but have not learned who they are in Christ. That is just natu-ral. The cosmetics industry, the clothing industry, and society as a whole revolve around the fear of rejection. We think we have to look our best, sound our best, do our best. We feel we have to perform to a certain standard or face rejection.

> *We fear men so much because we fear God so little.*

Have you ever felt like you have failed so miserably at something that all you wanted to do was go back into your room, home, or office, and shut the door, and never see another person because you feared their rejection? I have!

I remember a time when I was caught up in such a performance mode in all areas of my life. One Sunday I stood up to preach and the sermon was a bomb—not a little one, this was a nuclear bomb. It was horrible. I can remember feeling like a complete failure. My family remembers it too. I was so distraught that I told my family to go on to lunch without me. I walked straight back into my office, shut the door, and refused to see a soul. Why? Because I had failed, and I feared both the rejection of men and of God.

It is only through a breaking process (that I am still going through) that I am learning I am *"accepted in the Beloved"* (Ephesians 1:6). I am beginning to realize that no matter what I do, no matter how I fail (and I will fail), no matter what is going on in my life, I am accepted by God. And because I am accepted by God, I can face anyone—I do not have to fear rejection.

Suffering or pain is also feared by those without an understanding of God's grace. They worry about their health, injuries from an accident, the pain of illness, or the horrors of war.

Perhaps you have been diagnosed with a serious illness—even cancer. There is nothing wrong with feeling fear. It is part of being human. But the fear of cancer, as well as the fear of death, does not originate in the grace of God. When we fear circumstances, then we have lost sight of what it means to revere God.

Think, just for a moment, about tomorrow, or the next day, or the next week. Think of that thing of which you are afraid. Are you fearful of the pain and suffering that will come due to circumstances?

God will use our circumstances, even when painful, by providing comfort in order to teach us how to comfort others. *"Blessed be the God of all comfort; who comforts us in all our tribulation, that we may be able to comfort by the comfort where we ourselves are comforted of God"* (II Corinthians 1:3, 4). I believe that in time of tribulation God bestows a special grace to every believer as a gift to His people. The Scripture calls it "comfort." The word is used five times in this one reference.

Sometimes we look at others who are suffering and think, "You know Joe over there? He's a child of God, a believer, but he's really gone through a hard time. I don't know that I could have gone through what Joe has gone through."

Maybe a child has died in a family, and we think if that ever happened to us we could not stand it. But I have been with believers in times of great tragedy, and I have found that they have received a special grace. They have come through it by the grace of God. God has provided them His comfort. That is part of being in the New Covenant with God.

So where is our fear of pain and suffering coming from? Are we afraid of the very thing God is going to use in order that we might be a blessing to others?

Death is another real fear for nonbelievers. They have good reason to fear death. They *must* have an inner fear of being rejected by God. Self-professed atheists might cover it up and hide it, but those alienated from God can never feel calm about impending death. Although they deny it intellectually, deep in their hearts they know that ultimately they will stand before a holy God and answer to their Creator. They know they did not just arrive on this earth by chance or accident.

> ℂ
> *Death to believers is not the same as death to unbelievers.*
> ℂ

Even some believers fear impending death, but there is no reason because death to believers is not the same as death to unbelievers.

How does God look at the death of believers? *"Precious in the sight of the Lord is the death of His saints"* (Psalm 116:15 KJV). If we have been saved by the grace of God, if we know Jesus Christ as our Lord because we have placed our trust in Him, then there is no reason to fear death. It is a good thing. It is gain. It is a blessing. We can say along with Paul, *"To me to live is Christ, and to die is gain"* (Philippians 1:21).

Those without grace fear the future. They fear what is going to take place tomorrow. They are always worried about the economy, anxious about the next day, the next year, the next decade.

God has a plan for each one who is part of His family, and God has the power to fulfill that plan. Nothing can disrupt God's plans. *"A man's heart devises his way; but the Lord directs his steps"* (Proverbs 16:9). Nothing can prevent what God intends, what He prepares, what He plans, and what He will fulfill. Fear of the future does not come from God.

Unbelievers have a fear of man because they know their own hearts. They know down deep that humankind is intrinsically evil, not intrinsically good. In their ungraced hearts, they know what they are capable of, so they are watching for it in others. They often become paranoid, feel everyone is out to get them, and carefully watch their backs. They don't trust anyone because they know how untrustworthy they themselves are.

A believer *"may boldly say that the Lord is my helper, and I will not fear what man shall do unto me"* (Hebrews 13:6). But unbelievers do not have this confidence.

These are just five areas of fear that people *without* grace possess. But if you are like me, right now you might be thinking, "Wait a minute. I am *with* grace but I feel some of these fears."

WHERE DOES A BELIEVER'S FEAR COME FROM?

Even as believers, we may have fear in our hearts. We may fear others, the future, death, rejection, or circumstances which will bring suffering or pain.

God has not given us that fear, for the only good kind of fear is godly fear—fear that respects the Lord. So where do these fears come from if they do not come from God? Here are some possibilities.

A guilty conscience is sometimes evidence of fear in a believer. The Puritan, John Flavel, said, "Fear is the tax that conscience pays to guilt."

Let's say that, as a believer, you have never come to an understanding of what it means to be forgiven by God. You have never fully recognized the extent of Christ's atonement for you and your acceptance in the Beloved One.

At one time you may have understood how all of your sins were forgiven—past, present, and future. But now, you are in the midst of sin—unconfessed sin. As a person of grace, your sin is forgiven through the death of Christ, but because it remains unconfessed, there is something wrong within you. So, even as a believer, you are harboring sin—secret, private sins—that you desire no one else to know of. But you know that God knows.

Your unconfessed sin is destroying you emotionally and spiritually. You have a guilty conscience. Frankly, you ought to feel guilt if you have not acknowledged your sin.

Guilt is good in that the Holy Spirit will use it to convict us and drive us to the cross. After we come to the cross, realize the price Christ paid by His blood, and rest in His work in our behalf, any further guilt over our sin is not sent by the Holy Spirit. It is sent by Satan, the Deceiver, who sends guilt to cause us to be ashamed of who we are. Anytime we lose sight of the power of the cross, we will experience fear.

Some of us have absolutely blown it. Maybe we have ruined a relationship or even committed a crime. Even though we have admitted our sin and trust Christ, we live in constant guilt over the past. God does not send that spirit of guilt and fear. He sends His children a spirit of love, peace, and a sound mind (II Timothy 1:7).

We get rid of this wrong kind of fear by dealing with our past and knowing that our sin is nailed to the cross. If God will never bring it up again, why do we constantly bring it up ourselves? My prayer is that we will learn to be content in who we are, by the grace

Fear is the tax that conscience pays to guilt.

of God and the work of Jesus Christ, and that we will no longer live in the fear created by a conscience full of shame.

Faulty theology can also cause fear in the life of a believer. William Gurnall said, "We fear men so much because we fear God so little." Where there is *little* fear of God, there is a corresponding *great* fear of man.

Many professing Christians feel fear because they have never been taught the sovereignty and providence of God.

Or, they may have been taught it, but it is only in their heads and has not migrated to their hearts.

If there is fear in our lives, it could be because we have not seen who God is in His omniscience, His power, and His glory. We have a man-centered, man-oriented, faulty theology.

If we ever think that God is incapable of doing what He desires, we are in trouble. We have a limited God who is bound and unable to effect His own desires. Frankly, that is not much of a God at all.

But if we believe what the Scripture says about God—that He does as He pleases, always as He pleases, only as He pleases; if we see that all things work after the counsel of His will, that He has established His throne in the heavens, that His kingdom rules over all, and that nothing can annul the decrees of God; if we see God as sovereign and omnipotent; if our view of Him is high and lofty as the Scripture would have us see Him—then what do we have to fear?

A stronghold of sin can cause a believer to live in fear. The only way that kind of fear can be overcome is when we, by the grace of God, get rid of those strongholds. John Flavel said, "Let none but the servants of sin be the slaves of fear." *"The wicked flee when no man pursues, but the righteous are as bold as a lion"* (Proverbs 28:1).

> *Let none but the servants of sin be the slaves of fear.*

Right now some of you might be in bondage to a sin that you are clutching and not willing to give up. God is working in your conscience and through your circumstances to persuade you to give it up. But you are still clutching. It is like you have your hand in a jar grasping a gold coin. You will never be able to remove your hand from that jar until you let go of the coin. So it is with sin. Fear comes when we grasp sin and refuse to let go.

God will gently and lovingly break us of the bonds of sin. We will either be broken by the word of God, which is a hammer that breaks, or we will be broken by the work of God. It is our choice. We must never take lightly the teaching of God's word. A hardened heart is one that does not receive the word of God.

It might take time to break a stronghold of sin. If we are in the process of breaking and not yet broken, then we are still living in sin and will hurt. But when the process is finished, we will no longer be the slave of fear.

Pride will cause us to struggle with fear. Our continual concern for what others think is nothing but evidence of pride. Stop worrying about what people think! Just live your life.

Vance Havner said, "We are so afraid of being offensive that we are not effective." If we are more concerned about what other people think than about the truth, if we have pride, arrogance, or an ego that says, "I have to live up to every-

> *We are so afraid of being offensive that we are not effective.*

one else's expectations of me," then we are going to struggle with all kinds of fear.

May God strike at the root of the pride that makes us constantly fear what others think of us and teach us that we are everything we need to be because of Christ.

A performance mentality will produce an ungodly fear that will not let us rest in grace. Many believers experience fear because of a desire to perform and the feeling that they are not meeting their *own* expectations. They measure themselves against a standard by which they can never measure up. They suffer burnout because they are working so hard instead of resting in the work that Christ has already done.

Even worse, they expect others to perform to their self-imposed expectations. They become fretful, critical, judgmental, and irritable.

If we believe that our acceptance is based upon *our* works, rather than the work of Christ, we will always struggle with fear. But if we come to the place where we know that we are accepted because of His performance, rather than our self-imposed standards of behavior, then we can be protected from ourselves. We can be protected from our own self-righteousness. We can rest in Christ and even be free to fail.

So What Are You Afraid Of?

If you are a believer and there is ungodly fear in your life, God did not bring it. He accepts you with your fear, but your life is miserable because of it. Ask Him, by His grace, to help you discover why fear is present, to drive from you any spirit that smacks of the "fear of demons," and to give you the only kind of fear that is good—a healthy respect of who He is.

As long as we do not see the protection of God's providence, then we will be in bondage to ungodly fear. We will feel a loss of control and will try to manage that fear under our own power. Since the things we fear are beyond our power to control, then we might end up like the woman at the beginning of this chapter, rocking back and forth, afraid to leave the house. At the very least, we will sit and fret.

Even though there is no reason for us to fear anything in life, you may have lost a job or have other circumstances causing great anxiety about your future. We need not fear the future because the events of our lives have been ordained by God. But if you are in the middle of such fear, do not feel condemned. Realize that fear does not come from God, and remember that every child of God has the promise when crisis comes that if we cry out to our Father, God, He will be with us. He is there to protect us and will give us grace and comfort in times of need.

"For you have not received the spirit of bondage again to fear; but you have received the Spirit of adoption, whereby we cry, Abba, Father" (Romans 8:15). (In the next chapter, we will see more about what this spirit of adoption does for the believer.)

What are you afraid of—cancer, poverty, war, the future, rejection, death, or impending danger? God didn't give you that fear. Ask Him to take it away.

> *Though troubles assail*
> *And dangers affright*
> *Though friends should all fail*
> *And foes all unite.*
>
> *Yet one thing secures us*
> *Whatever the tide*
> *The Scripture answers us*
> *The Lord will provide.*
> John Newton

*It is interesting to notice that
as men and women know less and less
about a living spiritual experience
where God is Abba Father,
the more formal does their
worship become.*

Dr. D. Martin Lloyd Jones

Chapter 10
I Am Adopted

*Having predestinated us unto
the adoption of children by Jesus Christ to Himself,
according to the good pleasure of His will.*
Ephesians 1:5 (KJV)

When I was captain of my high school football team, we used to recite the Lord's Prayer before every game. It begins, *"Our Father, which art in heaven..."* (Luke 11:2b KJV).

Our coaches told us one day that it would no longer be legal for them to lead us in the Lord's Prayer. However, if the coaches were not present, the team could still recite the prayer. Since I was captain, it became my responsibility to lead the team in the Lord's Prayer.

As I led the team in prayer, I reminded them that not all of us have the right to call God "Father." Only those who have trusted Christ are those whom God has adopted as His children, and only His children have the right to call Him "Father."

What Does it Mean to Be Adopted by God?

Paul used the word *adoption* several times in his letters to the early Christian churches to describe a believer's relationship with the Lord. He tells believers that they have been adopted by God and have received the spirit of adoption:

God sent forth His Son to redeem them that were under the Law, that we might receive the adoption of sons (Galatians 4:4, 5).

Having predestinated us into the adoption of children by Jesus Christ to Himself, according to the good pleasure of His will (Ephesians 1:5).

When Paul used the term *adoption,* all of his hearers would understand what it meant because they were familiar with adoption proceedings. Adoption was customary in Roman times. The Romans had developed an elaborate civil ceremony by which children were adopted.

In the proceedings, the adopting family would gather, along with the judge, and the one who was being adopted. A beautiful, moving ceremony would then take place, which would end with an embrace of love. A similar ceremony occurred when a father publicly recognized that his natural-born son was old enough to receive Roman citizenship.

In the original Greek of the New Testament, the word *adopted* is a compound word: *huiothesia.* The first portion, *huios,* means "adult son." The second portion, *thesia,* means "to place or install." The word used for *adoption* in Scripture means "to place or install another as a son." If we are adopted by God, that means we have been "placed or installed" as a child of God.

PRIVILEGES OF ADOPTION

When, by the grace of God, we come to recognize our union with Jesus Christ, then we are saved, born again, regenerated, whatever you want to call it. We receive the spirit of adoption and are granted the following privileges of adoption.

God is our father. Believers have the special privilege and glory of being able to call God, "Father." *"And I will be a father to you, and you shall be my sons and daughters, says the Lord Almighty"* (II Corinthians 6:18).

"For you have not received the spirit of bondage again to fear; but you have received the spirit of adoption whereby we cry, Abba, Father" (Romans 8:15).

The word *abba* in this verse is one of a handful of Aramaic expressions adopted by the Greek-speaking church and left untranslated in the Greek text. The English translators of the Bible also left *abba* untranslated. *Abba* was an intimate family term used by sons and daughters to show both respect and endearment for a beloved father.

Paul knew there would be some reading his letter who would not understand the Aramaic word *abba,* so he used a second word, the Greek word *pater*, meaning father. That is why you have the double *father, father*.

No bondman or slave in Paul's time could ever utter the word *abba* to any free man. It was against the law. As believers we are not slaves—we are free. Paul says we have not received the spirit of bondage; we have received the spirit of adoption. As proof of this, we can legally call God *abba*, Father.

Many of us don't understand the significance of calling God, "Father," because we get caught up in the fact that our sins are forgiven and that we are pardoned. However, we could be pardoned and still be slaves—but we are *not* slaves. We are the chosen, adopted children of *abba*, *Father*, the Creator of the universe.

D. Martin Lloyd Jones says, "It is very interesting to notice that as men and women know less and less about a living, spiritual experience where God is *Abba* Father, the more formal does their worship become."

It is one thing to be pardoned by the king. It is quite another to be called the king's son or daughter. As a son or daughter, we ought not take for granted the special, awesome privilege of calling God, *abba*, *Father*. This is why I bristle at the idea of anyone without Christ reciting the Lord's Prayer. We have no privilege of calling our creator, "Father," unless we have the spirit of adoption through Jesus Christ. You might think that is hard-nosed of me but it is not. Only through Christ may we call God, "Father."

> ℘
>
> *Only through Christ may we call God, Father.*
>
> ℘

Scripture says that the reprobate, the unregenerate, or the lost, are children of wrath and disobedience. Jesus told the Pharisees and religious people in His day, who were not followers of Jehovah (especially not followers of Christ), *"You are of your father the devil, and the lusts of your father you will do"* (John 8:44a).

Dr. John Gill says:

> Calling God Father is a blessing of grace which exceeds other blessings; as redemption, pardon, justification and sanctification, a man may be redeemed out of a state of slavery by a king's ransom; may be pardoned by his prince, and may be acquitted from high crimes laid to his charge. And yet not be a king's son. If adopted and taken into his family it must be another and distinct act of royal favor.

We have free access to God. We are invited to go to Him and approach Him. We have been given this privilege by the spirit of adoption. *"Let us come boldly unto the throne of grace, that we may obtain mercy, and find grace to help in time of need"* (Hebrews 4:16).

Many other religions and many Christians give their leader, pastor, or priest the title of "Father." Some believe they must go through a mediator, either here on earth or a saint in heaven. But I believe a full understanding of the spirit of adoption means that we have the special privilege of free access to our Father in heaven.

I read that Donald Trump, the wealthy millionaire from New York, allows no one to interrupt his meetings except his children. He can be in a most important board meeting, but his children have free access to the boardroom and can walk right in to where their father is sitting. That is the kind of access that we have to our Heavenly Father. We have free access to His throne room.

Do you fully realize the significance of this? When we face our puny little problems, our high and mighty God loves for us to come into His presence expressing our needs to Him, the One who loves us. If you are hurting, go to your Father. I'm sometimes amazed when people who are struggling come to me with their problem, and I ask them, "Have you gone to the Lord with this matter?" They say, "Oh, well...I didn't think about that." Well, why not?

Sometimes the reason we don't go to the Lord with our problems is because we feel guilty or unworthy. We feel we don't measure up. But if our son or daughter ever wanted to come talk to us, would we keep him or her out? No. How much more does our Heavenly Father love us?

Protection is provided to those who are adopted.

Jesus said, *"If a son shall ask bread of any of you that is a father, will he give him a stone? Or if he ask a fish, will he for a fish give him a serpent? Or if he shall ask an egg will he offer him a scorpion? If you then, being evil, know how to give good gifts unto your children; how much more shall your Heavenly Father give the Holy Spirit to them that ask Him?"* (Luke 11:11-13)

Do you know to whom Jesus is speaking? He is speaking to His disciples. Do you see what he says of them? He says "If you then being *evil*. . ." That ought to persuade us that we don't need to convince ourselves, or others, that we are good in order to approach our Father, God.

If you are afraid, then cry out to Him, *"Abba,* Father." The protection and provision provided to us by Him is given out of this spirit of adoption that the Lord gives to His children. Look back to Chapter Nine to see that a believer need not fear rejection, suffering, pain, death, the future, or what others may do to him.

When we are children of God we know our Father's ways. God reveals to us, by His spirit, direction for our lives.

If you were to invite my father and me to dinner and sit us down at a big plate of vittles, I promise you I know what my father will do once the blessing has been said. How do I know? Because I've seen him do it for years.

Here is what he does. After we say "Amen," he picks up his glass of tea, takes two sips, and sets it down. Every single time he will do this. In fact, I even do it myself. When "Amen" is said I also pick up my glass, take two sips, and set it down. (I don't even know I am doing it.)

How do I know what my father does? I'm his son, I know his ways. You wouldn't know that about him, would you?

The one who has the spirit of adoption knows and loves God, and knows and loves God's ways. The natural man does not. The natural man not only does not know or love God's ways but thinks they are foolish. *"But the natural man receives not the things of the Spirit of God. For they are foolishness to him; neither can he know them, because they are spiritually discerned"* (I Corinthians 2:14).

In Greek the word *foolish* is *moros*, from which we get our word *moron*. This same word was used by Jesus when He said, *"If the salt becomes tasteless [moros] it is good for nothing, but to be cast out and trampled upon"* (Matthew 5:13). It is translated *tasteless* in this verse, but it's the same word that is used for *foolish* in Paul's letter to the Corinthians. The man without Christ, the natural man, does not welcome the things of God, for they are "tasteless" and "moronic" to him because they can only be spiritually discerned.

God is concerned and cares for our future. As adopted children we are heirs of God. We are joint heirs with Christ (Romans 8:17). As children of God, our Heavenly Father guarantees a future full of loving concern, care, and compassion. He will watch over us.

> *Calling God Father is a blessing of grace which exceeds other blessings.*

The events of our life have been ordained by God. He has plans for our future, and nothing can disrupt those plans. It does not depend upon *our* faithfulness or upon *our* obedience. It depends upon *His* faithfulness.

God's concern and watchcare over our future will not allow us to be involved in particular sins that are destructive. God will not allow them to continue, for He cares for us. He does not hate us, nor is He angry with us. Sin is destructive, so God has chosen to separate His children from their sins.

When we become involved in sin, He will chastise us, but never in anger. He is not vindictive with a believer. When He sees a destructive pattern of life, He gently and lovingly will move into the realm of that child who is sinning and bring that child to repentance. The promise is, *"He who has begun a good work in you will perform it until the day of Jesus Christ"* (Philippians 1:6b).

As God's children, we are free. *"Jesus said unto him, Then are the children free,"* (Matthew 17:26). *"If the Son shall make you free, you shall be free indeed"* (John 8:36).

If we are adopted by the Spirit, if we are children of God, then we are not slaves—we are free. We are free from the law, because we are sons and daughters—not slaves. Christ has fulfilled the Law on our behalf. Do not allow anyone to take this liberty from you.

> *We are free because we are sons and daughters, not slaves.*

How far does freedom go? It goes as far as the boundaries set up in the New Testament allow: no drunkenness, adultery, idolatry, murder, envying, etc. (Galatians 5:19-21). But great freedom is found within these parameters, including freedom to love and freedom to forgive.

In Chapter Eight we looked at how we are free from the law and all the things that bind us up in the religious world. We are free from the traditions of men. We don't need the traditions and rituals of men to worship God. We are free to worship Him according to the dictates of our conscience and the word of God. I pity the person who is so bound up in legalism and rituals that he thinks he must perform a certain way, act a certain way, do a certain thing, or say a certain prayer to be pleasing to God. He thinks he has to have a prescribed "quiet time," do his "daily Bible readings," say fifteen "Hail Marys," use the proper "prayer language," walk down an aisle, tithe. These might all be good disciplines and help our focus, but we must never think that we do these in order for God to bless us.

GLORIOUS LIBERTY IN THE WORLD TO COME

> *Creation itself will also be set free from its slavery to corruption into the freedom of the glory of the children of God. For we know that the whole creation groans and suffers the pains of childbirth together unto now. Not only this, but also we ourselves having the firstfruits of the Spirit, even we ourselves groan within ourselves waiting eagerly for our adoption as sons, the redemption of our body.* (Romans 8:21-23)

The full understanding of our adoption will be seen at the coming of the Lord Jesus Christ. We can only see vaguely now. We are shown a truth, but it's like we're looking through an opaque glass. We see it, we want to believe it, but we can't fully comprehend it.

When Jesus Christ comes in all His glory, the truth that you are now hearing—that we are a child of God, loved by Him, adopted by Him, cared for by Him, protected by Him —will be displayed in all of its grandeur. It will be true of us for eternity to come because we have received the spirit of adoption.

I AM ADOPTED

Even if everyone else in this world rejects us, we have One who will never reject us. If your wife rejects you or your husband walks out on you; if somebody abandons you, or stays with you, but rejects you every day of their life—if they don't like the way you talk, the way you act, or the things you do; if they don't receive you and don't accept you—you still have the One who has chosen you, adopted you, and loves you.

I know this is easy to say and hard to put into practice. I know rejection hurts for a season, but our happiness is not dependent upon what other people do. It is dependent upon the faithfulness of our Heavenly Father. He does not love us because of what we can be. He loves us as we are because of who He is.

We can focus on the truth that we are adopted by God. We are His. He has reached down by His Holy Spirit and given us the spirit of adoption whereby we may call Him, *abba,* Father.

Every adopted child is a chosen child. When God chose us for adoption He put us in an eternal relationship with Him. Along with that relationship come all the privileges and glory of being a child of the King.

Providence means God preserves,
governs, directs, and guides
all creatures whom He has made.
His special providence
is that care over those whom
He loves in a special manner.

Dr. John Gill

Chapter 11
I Am Guided

A man's heart plans his way,
but the Lord directs his steps.
Proverbs 16:9

C. S. Lewis tells the following story in his essay, "The Efficacy of Prayer":

> Some years ago I got up one morning intending to have my hair cut in preparation for a visit to London, and the first letter I opened made it clear I need not go to London. So I decided to put the haircut off too. But then there began the most unaccountable little nagging in my mind, almost like a voice saying, "Get it cut all the same, Go and get it cut." In the end I could stand it no longer. I went. Now my barber at that time was a fellow-Christian and a man of many troubles whom my brother and I had some-times been able to help. The moment I opened his shop door he said, 'Oh, I was praying you might come today.' And in fact if I had come a day or so later I should have been of no use to him.[1]

Was it just coincidence that Lewis came in on the day the barber had prayed? Was it the barber's "lucky" day? Or was C. S. Lewis guided there by God as an answer to the barber's prayer? And was the barber guided to pray that Lewis might come that day?

WE ARE GUIDED BY THE PROVIDENCE OF GOD

To be guided is to be led. There is an idea of dependence either upon someone else or some kind of plan, or chart, or guidebook.

How are we guided by the providence of God? How should it affect the way we face our day-to-day circumstances? What should His providence mean to us? How should it make us feel? What should it make us do?

Unbelievers can only attribute the direction of their lives to luck or to chance. Some go to astrologers, palm readers, or fortune tellers in their quest for guidance. But a believer knows there is something far more grand than luck or chance guiding his or her life. A believer rests in God's providence.

"Providence," according to Dr. John Gill, "means God preserves, governs, directs, and guides all creatures whom He has made. His special providence is that care over those whom He loves in a special manner."

God did not put the universe in motion and then just sit back and let us flounder, with our lives guided only by our own finite wills and intellects. *"God works all things after the counsel of His own will"* (Ephesians 1:11). *"A man's heart plans his way, but the Lord directs his steps"* (Proverbs 16:9).

WE THINK WE DON'T WANT TO BE GUIDED

Today's average American struggles with the idea that we are guided. We are a culture of self-made men in charge of our own destinies. We get a little uncomfortable around those who say, "I am guided."

Even some believers trust that God is in control of their final destiny, but are not looking to Him for daily guidance (unless they are in trouble or having difficulty deciding which path to take). Most of the time we go about our daily living with no perception of the guidance and providence of God. There are several reasons we think we don't want to be guided by God.

We want control. When we desire to have *self-control,* it shows that we don't trust anyone but ourselves to be in charge of our lives. We also try to control the lives of those around us. We become "control freaks," and if we continue, we will find it to be very stressful.

How can we say we trust God with our salvation if we don't trust Him to guide our lives? Is His arm too short or His strong right hand too weak to guide us? Can we really do better ourselves?

We are fearful of God's leadership. We are fearful of allowing ourselves to be guided because we are afraid if we follow Him, then He will surely make us missionaries to China, or want us to live in a convent, or force us to knock on doors sharing the gospel.

We don't want to lose our identity. We think if we were to let God guide us that He might make us weird. If we were to consult His guidance about our wardrobes, He might make us dress like Jesus dressed. We might all be wearing robes and sandals and preaching on the streets.

> *Providence means God preserves, governs, directs, and guides all . . .*

Whom Do You Want to Be Your Guide?

So we think we don't want to be guided. We want to be free to guide ourselves.

Are we qualified for the task? What makes us think we are qualified to control our own destinies? Are we wiser than God? When we try to be in control, don't we make a huge mess of things? Or, if not a mess, aren't our outcomes usually less than we expected? Who is better qualified to guide our lives—our finite selves or the infinite Creator?

Are we more compassionate than God? We have the idea if we let God guide us, then He will make our lives miserable—long faces, proper behavior, no more fun.

What if our child came to us one day and said, "Dad, I've been thinking it over and I've decided from now on I am going to do everything you tell me to do." If our child told us that, would we take away all of his toys, tell him to live in a closet, and only feed him broccoli three times a day? Of course not. How much more compassion will our Heavenly Father show to us?

Whose plan is best? What are the plans and goals you have set for your life? Can you map out your life better than He who planned the universe? Could you write a better *auto*biography than the biography He has written for you?

Sometimes God sends circumstances our way that are not to our liking. Like Job, we accuse God of mismanagement. Here is God's answer to Job when Job questioned God's guidance of his life:

> *Who is this that darkens counsel by words without knowl-edge? . . .Where were you when I laid the foundations of the earth? . . .Or shut up the sea with doors, when it broke forth . . . Have you commanded the morning since your days; and caused the dayspring to know his place?* (Job 38:2, 4a, 8a, 12)

When Job saw the sovereignty and omnipotence of God, he repented. God restored Job, and *"the Lord blessed the latter part of Job's life more than his beginning"* (Job 42:12a).

Even after we begin to understand that God is guiding our lives, if things don't happen *when* we expect them to, we get impatient. Like Abraham, we see time slipping away and decide to take things into our own hands (Genesis 16). We try to produce outcomes ourselves instead of waiting for God's perfect timing.

God's Providence Is Immediate and Mediate

Immediate providence is obtaining results without any intervening agency, medium, or means. God sometimes governs, guides, and preserves without the work of any means. He works directly to bring about results. God has the power to care for His creation and those whom He loves by simply speaking the word, and it will be accomplished.

For instance, when He created the world, He made the earth fruitful though it had never rained. How can God do that? He can because He is all-powerful. He can speak the word, and it will come to pass. *"He upholds all things by the word of His power"* (Hebrews 1:3).

When Moses was on Mount Sinai, God sustained and supported his body (Exodus 34:28) without food, water, or nourishment because God used immediate providence. Normally, a man's body is sustained by eating, but God sustained Moses without the means of food.

When God caused the waters to part in the Red Sea (Exodus 14:21), He caused a wind to blow, and the waters parted. Normally, it would take some physical means, like a dam, to part waters.

Mediate providence is when God uses natural means to accomplish His purposes. Sometimes in Scripture God would give victory to small armies over large ones. The small army of Israelites would have the means, which were weapons, but it was God, in His providence, who chose to give them victory over their more powerful enemies.

Many of God's people were sustained miraculously by God through natural means such as food. God provided food for the Israelites as they wandered in the wilderness. Jesus fed over five thousand people with loaves and fishes.

We usually take for granted that our lives are sustained by natural means. We take for granted that our bodies are sustained by food, that it rains to produce crops, or that we will have the things we need to exist. We take for granted it is God, using the natural means of sending rain, who makes the earth fruitful.

If we recognize that God in His mercy, His love, His grace, and His providence, is guiding every step of our lives, then we will stop trusting in the means of life and begin trusting in the One who gives them. Every small blessing becomes a great one because God has given it. We no longer will take

> *Stop trusting in the means of life—begin trusting in the One who gives them.*

for granted what we have because we know it has been given to us by God. All we need to do is give Him the glory.

PROVIDENCE MAY BE ORDINARY OR EXTRAORDINARY

Ordinary providence is seen in the laws established by God: laws of gravity, laws of the harvest, laws of animal instinct, etc. According to the law of gravity, if we jump off a high building, we will fall. According to the laws of harvest, the more we sow, the more we reap; what we sow is what we reap; and we reap more than we sow.

God has given different laws of instinct to different animals. Salmon will always swim a certain direction during mating season. Some birds will fly south or fly north according to the seasons.

Extraordinary providence is when God goes out of His common way and performs miraculous operations that seem to be against ordinary, established laws.

Moses struck a rock, and water flowed from the rock (Exodus 17:6). By nature, we would think that could not occur, but God can work in His providence in extraordinary ways.

An axe head floated (II Kings 6:6). According to natural laws, an iron axe head should sink. This incident shows God's care and provision even in the insignificant events of everyday life.

The food in the widow's barrel at Zarephath should not have lasted but a day. Yet God, in His extraordinary providence, stretched that supply of food out over many days (I Kings 17:8-16).

God, in His providence, is able to do extraordinary or miraculous things. But that does not mean that if we are sick we should not go to a doctor, take medicine, or go through surgery. One of the laws in the healing process is to take care of a disease in every way possible in order to be healed. Medical procedures are part of the providence of God. Any faith-healing movement that says we lack faith in God if we go to a doctor and use medical means has no understanding of a sovereign God.

At times, God may choose to use extraordinary means. He may choose to do things that are contrary to natural laws. Even though God uses medical science, there are times when nothing medically can be done to heal a person. But God, by the word of His power, may heal that person. He has done it, and He can do it. But it is up to Him to make that decision.

GOD'S PROVIDENCE IS UNIVERSAL AND SINGULAR

Universal providence concerns God's upholding act preserving all things that are created. It is a general providence. The Scripture says He upholds *all* things by the word of His power (Hebrews 1:3).

Singular providence is concerned with each individual, especially with rational creatures and their actions. Every part of His creation has special interest to Him. Isaiah 40:26 tells us that God knows by name all of the stars in the heavens.

> *He upholds the entire world but He also sustains and upholds me.*

A sparrow does not fall but that God has ordained it. He knows it. His providence rules. How much more shall we, His people, have the concern, care, guidance, and protection of the Almighty God.

To say that His providence is universal and singular, means He upholds the entire world by the word of His power, but He also sustains and upholds *me*.

God's Providence Is Common and Special

Common providence is that which belongs to the whole world and all creatures in it. *"The Lord is good to all and His tender mercies are over all His works"* (Psalm 145:9).

Special providence is that which concerns the church of God in all ages. According to Scripture, God has a special care, a special governing, a special providence, a special guidance for His people, the church. *"God is the Savior over all men, especially of those that believe"* (I Timothy 4:10).

God Guides His People

Whatever is in our heart, whatever plans we have, we begin to make our plans and devise the means by which we will obtain our goals; but if God, in His providence, will direct our steps. If we want to do a certain thing because our heart is in it, but in God's watchcare, guidance, and providence it is not what is best for us, God will close a door in front of us or place a hedge about us. When Paul had a desire to move east, God, in His providence, purpose, and plan, moved Paul west (Acts 16:7).

When some say to me, "Wade, it is so difficult for me to know the will of God. It is so hard for me to know God's best for my life," I want to reply, "Wait a minute. Do you not believe that God is able to show you His best? Do you not believe that God is able to design and orchestrate your life, and order your steps, and lead you to the best? Do you think

God is so limited in His authority and power that He is unable to guide you down the best path?"

God is good to His people. In His providence, He leads and guides. His will is not lost. It is made plain in His Word. Sure, there are times when we want to go against His Word and the principles that are found there. But God, in His loving providence, has a way of bringing us back because sin is never best for God's people.

ARE YOU FEARFUL OF FOLLOWING?

If we don't recognize that we are guided, we will have problems with how we face the future, how we live in the present, and how we regard the past.

We will have anxiety about the future if we prefer to trust ourselves rather than God's guidance. We will be bound up in anxiety about decisions. We will constantly worry that we are doing the wrong thing or be so caught up in indecision that we fail to do anything at all.

We are unable to appreciate the present when we don't focus on God's providence. We have little joy and peace. We grumble and complain. We look at our circumstances with disappointment and live in a fantasy world of unrealistic expectations.

The focus is on ourselves and the weight of our decisions. We aren't able to revel in the moment because we have nagging doubts about whether we are doing the right thing.

We regret the past. If we resist the notion that we are guided, we keep looking back to the past and what might have been. We second-guess our past decisions and keep thinking "what if" or "if only." "If only I had done this, said that, taken that job, or moved to that town, then I would be happy."

FOLLOWING WITH CONFIDENCE

If we say, "I am guided," then we can face the future with confidence, enjoy the present, and put the past behind us.

We can have faith in the future. If we know we are guided by God's providence, then, although we don't know what the future holds, we know who holds the future. We can make decisions with confidence and peace.

What about times when difficult choices are ahead? You might say, "I just don't know what my future holds. I just don't understand where I should go, what I should do. I don't know the will of God for my life."

My reply to you is, "Delight yourself in Him, and He will guide." Don't get so caught up in having to discover God's will. He is going to guide. His providence will move you down the right path.

Then you might say, "But I want to do what is God's best for me." When you follow God's principles, don't worry about what is God's best. If you are following His principles, He will give you the best.

Let's think of an extreme decision. Let's imagine you are thinking of marriage, but there are two individuals who have come into your life who want to marry you.

What are the principles of marriage in Scripture? One principle is not to be unequally yoked (II Corinthians 6:14). Let's assume that both potential spouses are believers. Another principle is parental authority (Exodus 20:12). Let's say that your parents like both of the individuals—there's nothing wrong with either. Your parents would not prohibit marriage to one or the other. What is another principle? Ask the Lord for wisdom. Let's suppose you do all of that and still don't know which one you should marry.

So what do you do? You have followed Biblical principles but still can't decide. You know what my advice would be? Flip a coin!

You know why? You can flip a coin knowing that God will guide you in what is best for your life. *"For the Lord shows Himself strong in the behalf of them whose heart is perfect toward Him"* (II Chronicles 16:9).

We can have peace in the present. When we trust in God's guidance, then we are free to enjoy life with confidence and joy and to trust in God, ourselves, and others.

We will not have peace in our marriage relationships if we are wondering whether we have God's best partner for us. We cannot be satisfied with our partners if we think God had someone better for us out there. But if we trust God's providence in our relationships, we can rest

> *When you follow God's principles, He will give you the best.*

assured that we have the best. Don't doubt it. Enjoy your spouse and be grateful for him or her. Once we see that our lives have been guided by God, then we can consider our mates as gifts from God to us.

We can go about our daily lives with peace and patience knowing *"that all things work together for good to them that love God, to them who are the called according to his purpose"* (Romans 8:28). This powerful promise also gives us patience with others to let God work things in His timing in their lives as well.

Just relax, don't fret, be anxious for nothing. *"Be still and know that I am God"* (Psalm 46:10). This does not mean stupidity, insensibility, stoical apathy, or inactivity. But rather, to be still, quiet, and easy as opposed to being anxious and fretful. *"Fret not yourself"* (Psalm 37:1, 7, 8).

We must get over the past. We must put our mistakes behind us and not be too proud of our successes. The past is past. Get over it. Sure we have made mistakes—sure we have sinned. Even the bad and even our sinfulness can be used by God for our ultimate good.

If we made some choices in the past that we are particularly proud of, we must put that pride behind us. We did not do one thing to help God's perfect will come to pass. God's will has been accomplished, is being accomplished, and will always be accomplished. Our story is *"His* Story."

CONSTANTLY MAKE REFERENCE TO THE WILL OF GOD

Even though we often hear that we should just "name it and claim it," and "by faith go and never doubt," I believe it is more biblical and honors God more to make plans but always say, "By God's providence we will do this."

Make plans—go ahead and make preparations. Do the desire of your heart recognizing that, although we make plans, God directs our steps. So that all along the way we say, *"If the Lord wills, we shall live and do this and that"* (James 4:15). But if the Lord wills it not, then we say, *"It is the Lord. Let Him do what seems good"* (I Samuel 3:18).

But Where Might He Guide Me?

Now you might read this and think, "Okay, I see that I need to depend on God's guidance. If I let myself be guided by Him, then the path should be easy. If I follow Him, He will surely make it all smooth sailing for me." But when we look at the lives of some godly people around us, we see that their lives are not without problems and struggles. Some of the great saints and martyrs of the past who followed the guidance of God suffered great persecution. When we see this, we may become reluctant and fearful.

> *"I will take the Ring," he said, "though I do not know the way."²*

We might feel like Frodo in *The Lord of the Rings*. Although God is never mentioned in *The Lord of the Rings*, His providence is one of the underlying motifs of the book.

Frodo Baggins was a Hobbit. Hobbits were not much given to travel. They preferred to live in peace and quiet in the security of the Shire. But that all changed for Frodo when he inherited a mysterious ring from his uncle, Bilbo. It became apparent that, for the safety of the Shire, Frodo must leave the comfort and ease of his Hobbit hole and begin a dangerous quest.

Even though Frodo was sure this was his destiny, he was reluctant to leave because he knew it would mean exile and "a flight from danger into danger." He wanted to see the road ahead and to have a clear-cut understanding of his mission. He said to Gandalf:

> "For where am I to go? And by what shall I steer? What is to be my quest? Bilbo went to find a treasure, there and back again; but I go to lose one, and not return, as far as I can see."

"But you cannot see very far,' said Gandalf. 'Neither
can I." . . .
"But in the meantime what course am I to take?"
"Towards danger; but not too rashly, nor too straight."

Frodo asked the questions that many ask when pondering
the paths down which their lives are guided. He said:

> ". . . I am not made for perilous quests. I wish I
> had never seen the ring! Why did it come to me? Why
> was I chosen?"
> "Such questions cannot be answered," said Gandalf.
> "You may be sure that it was not for any merit that others
> do not possess: not for power or wisdom, at any rate. But
> you have been chosen, and you must therefore use such
> strength and heart and wits as you have."
> "But I have so little of any of these things!"

A surprising thing then happened to Frodo. As he was
telling Gandalf how small, and uprooted, and desperate he
felt, "a great desire to follow Bilbo flamed up in his heart . . .
It was so strong that it overcame his fear."[3]

We may be guided in easy paths and never be called upon
to "leave the Shire," or we may be guided to a dangerous
quest. We, like Frodo, want to see the end of the quest and
have all things work out the way that seems best to us. But
all we need to know about our quest is that the God who
loves us is working things out for His glory and the good of
His people. In whatever type of path He sets out for us, we
can rest assured that He will give us the desire to follow.

When we know that, as a believer, "I am guided," then we
can be happy in who we are. We can be still, quiet, and easy.
We don't need to be anxious because we are resting in God's
providence. We can hold our peace. We don't need to murmur and complain, but give thanks for everything, for God is
in control.

There is no way we can be holy.
Our holiness is Christ.

A. W. Pink

Chapter 12
I Am Holy

According as He hath chosen us in Him
before the foundation of the world,
that we should be holy and without blame before Him in love.
Ephesians 1:4 (KJV)

Jim Ryan was the first human to run the mile in under four minutes. Years before he did it, people said it was impossible for a human being to run faster than a four-minute mile. Jim Ryan fooled them all. He did what some called the impossible.

It is possible for Wade Burleson to go out and run a four-minute mile. But it is an *impossible* possibility. My body may want to do it; scientists may say that I can do it; but I know for a fact that it is impossible for me to run the four-minute mile (even though it is a possibility).

If you wanted me to work on your car, that also would be an impossible possibility.

We are going to look at the possibility that we can be holy by our activity or by obedience to the law. It is possible. But it is an impossible possibility.

THE BIBLE SAYS IT IS POSSIBLE FOR US TO BE HOLY

Many verses show it is possible to be holy, righteous, and accepted by God due to good works. Such as:

To them who by patient continuance in well doing seek for glory, honor, and immortality, [God will give] *eternal life* (Romans 2:7).

God will give glory, honor, and peace to every man that works good (Romans 2:10).

The doers of the law are justified in the eyes of God (Romans 2:13).

That is the possibility presented to us. If we obey the law, if we do good "by patient continuance," then we are holy. We will be treated by God as sinless, we will be right with him—righteous and holy. Since these verses indicate that it is possible to be right with God by good works, then we might resolve to try harder, to shape up, to do better, to give it our best shot in order to measure up. We become determined to obey the law to the best of our ability.

THE REST OF THE STORY

The problem is that if we stop with those verses, then we haven't heard the rest of the story. We lose track of Paul's train of thought because he goes on to show us it is an impossible possibility for us to make ourselves holy.

Paul continues in Romans 3:23 to say, *"all have sinned and come short of the glory of God."* No one measures up. There is no one who *"in patient continuance always does well"* (Romans 2:7). Therefore, it is impossible for anyone to be holy "by deeds of the law."

Since it is impossible for us to be holy by our own obedience, Paul reveals to us a holiness that comes apart from the law—a righteousness that is not obtained by our obedience to the law. He proclaims the wonderful Gospel of Jesus Christ:

> *But now the righteousness of God without the law is manifested, being witnessed by the law and the prophets; Even the righteousness of God which is by faith of Jesus Christ unto all and upon all them that believe; for there is no difference.*
> (Romans 3:21, 22 KJV)

There is a righteousness that is not based upon our obedience to the law—a righteousness based upon the obedience of Jesus. We cannot earn this righteousness or holiness by our own activity. It comes to us by faith in the good work of Jesus Christ. This is the gospel message.

TRYING HARDER

However, the vast majority of the world is under the delusion that if they simply try their hardest to obey the law of God, then God will really be happy with them.

I once watched a distinguished, good-looking gentleman preaching on Christian television. He was very polished and presented his message very well. The auditorium was nearly full. For about twenty-five minutes, I listened to him preach on the same verses that I have just shown you in Romans.

In a very gentle, gracious, patient kind of way, he was chastising listeners for not measuring up to the law of God. He rebuked us for not doing our best in following after good, in seeking to glorify God by delving into the word, in finding out what He would have us do, and in following through with discipline and integrity, seeking God's glory and

His honor. By the time he was done, I was absolutely worn out.

Sadly, this preacher missed the very essence of what the Bible teaches. Even though Paul says that "by the deeds of the law" we are made right with God, and that "by patient continuance in well-doing" God accepts, favors, and blesses us; he comes to the conclusion that this is impossible for us. We can't do it. If we miss that, we will wear ourselves out.

Professing to Love the Law of God Does Not Make Us Holy

God chose the Jews to be His people, revealed Himself to them through His word, and gave them His law which is found in the Old Testament or the Old Covenant. In the Old Testament, God told Adam, Noah, Moses, and many others what He expected from them.

The Jews loved the fact that they had His law, His word, and delved deeply into it. They believed it was possible to be right with God by obeying God's law. The law promised blessing and eternal life if perfectly obeyed.

Because they had the word of God and the law of God, the Jews considered themselves better than the Gentiles. But, in his letter to the Romans, Paul compared the Jews to those Gentiles who were without the Covenant and the Law. Paul said:

> *For there is no respect of persons with God. For as many as have sinned without law* [the Gentiles] *shall also perish without law: and as many as have sinned in the law* [the Jews] *shall be judged by the law."* (Romans 2:11, 12 KJV)

God shows no favoritism—He is impartial in his judgment. The Jews, who have the Law, will receive the same judgment as the Gentiles, who don't have the Law. The Gentiles will perish, and the Jews will perish too.

We, as believers, have the laws of God, the revelation of His will. But just because we have the word of God, and just because we say we love the word of God, and just because we delve deeply into Bible study, that does not make us holy.

MEASURING UP

You say, "That's fine with me, because I'm not just hearing the word of God, I'm doing it. I'm a practicing, holy, spiritual, abundant-life believer!" I say to you, "No, you are not!"

You see, God is impeccable in his holiness. Fellowship with God requires absolute perfection. Jesus said, *"Be therefore perfect, even as your Father in heaven is perfect"* (Matthew 5:48). That is the standard of the law—perfection. The law promises favor, blessing, and life from God if we obey it perfectly.

> &
> *Fellowship with God requires absolute perfection.*
> &

The law promises punishment and condemnation if violated once—just once. *"For whosoever shall keep the whole law and yet offend in one point, he is guilty of it all"* (James 2:10). *Perfect* obedience is the only thing that qualifies as real holiness.

You say, "That's impossible!"

It is—but can't God demand perfection? He himself is perfect. He created us. Can't He say of us, "I demand you to perfectly obey the law"? Yes, He can. He is God. But our holiness will never measure up to the standard of God. This cuts the knees from under our self-righteousness.

You say, "But isn't it good to love the law of God and the word of God?" Of course it is. I love the word of God. I've invested my life in studying it and teaching it. But just because I say, "I love the word of God," and study it, and read it, and learn Greek and Hebrew, and have an extensive library of commentaries on the Bible, it doesn't mean squat.

We often look at others who aren't in a Bible study as we are, or don't love God's word as much as we do, and think we're better than they. But, loving the word of God doesn't make us holy.

PERFORMING THE LETTER OF GOD'S LAW DOESN'T MAKE US HOLY

I know many Christians who spend their lives trying to convince people of the importance of being holy before God by obeying His laws.

"God's laws" vary from church to church. If we want to perform to the letter of God's law in order to be holy, we must ask a question: "What is God's law?"

We are not the first to ask that question. An attorney came to Jesus in order to test his orthodoxy and asked, *"Master, what is the greatest commandment of the law?"* (Matthew 22:36)

Jesus answered: *"You shall love the Lord your God with all your heart, all your soul and all your mind. This is the first and greatest commandment. The second is like it: You shall love your neighbor as yourself. On these two commandments hang all the law and the prophets"* (Matthew 22:37-40).

I can just hear some of you say, "Aha! There it is! I get it! That's the law of God. I'm to love Him with all my mind, my soul, and my heart, and my neighbor as myself. That's it, all right. I'm going to do it. I'm going to give it my best shot. I'm going to try to measure up."

Consider what Walter Marshall has to say in *The Gospel Mystery of Sanctification Opened*:

> Some are so near the kingdom of God that though they continue in a natural state, they are convinced of the spirituality of the law. To them, this law binds us principally to love God with all our heart, soul, mind and strength, and to love our neighbor as ourselves. . . . So they struggle . . . to perform every known duty of the law with their whole heart and soul, as the law demands. They are so active and intent in their devout practice, that they over-work their natural strength, and so fervent in their zeal, that they are ready even to kill their bodies with very severe fastings, and with other cruel activities, that they may kill their sinful lusts. They are strongly convinced that holiness is absolutely necessary to salvation . . . yet they have never been enlightened to the mystery of the gospel, to know that a new state in Christ is necessary to a new life; therefore they labour in vain to reform their natural state, instead of getting above it in Christ. And some of these . . . do at last fall miserably into despair of ever attaining to holiness, and turn to wallow in the mire of their lusts, or are fearfully swallowed up with horror of conscience.

How Do We Love God?

When we place ourselves under obligation to love God, we try to devise ways to measure the depth of our love. We orchestrate our own list of laws. We often define how to love God by things we do and don't do. We say: "If you do this or don't do that, it means that you love God with all your heart, your mind, and your soul." How foolish.

We Baptists are the absolute worst at this. "We don't dance, we don't chew, and we don't go with girls who do." We *don't do* a lot of things. We also have a list of things *we must do*. We *must* be in church every time the doors are open.

At the very least, we must be there every Sunday morning, Sunday night, and Wednesday night—not to mention all the revivals, conferences, seminars, Bible studies, and special meetings in between.

We even add attitudes to our list of laws. We make a law out of *"patient continuance in well doing"* (Romans 2:7). We expect to be doing good all the time, without flinching, always putting our face to the flint, and always doing the right thing in thought, action, or deed. Besides all the *do's* and *don'ts,* we must continually examine ourselves to see if we are sincere and genuine when we perform our duties.

Then we start looking around to see if others are doing the same! If others aren't complying with our list, we, the *self*-righteous, condemn them.

When we get caught up in this type of legalism, we have lost sight of the Gospel message of a holiness that is apart from us, that comes from Jesus Christ. We don't see that the law of loving God and neighbor demands absolute perfec-tion, and that even professing Christians do not perform to the letter of the law.

> *To be made holy by our own good works is an impossible possibility.*

If it were possible to "love God with all your heart and soul and your neighbor as yourself," we would not need a Savior.

Who Is Good?

On the other hand, there are those who are not concerned about God's law at all. Many in the United States no longer go to church. Some say, "What good is church? What do I need church for? Look, I'm as good as those neighbors of mine who go to church all the time."

Some believe that humankind is intrinsically good. Therefore, anything they do that might seem bad is just a result of circumstances. They blame the culture, their parents, or society for their sins. They don't need the outdated authority of Scripture with its absolute values because they believe all actions are relative. Their conscience is their guide.

> *For when the Gentiles, which have not the law, do by nature the things contained in the law, these, having not the law, are a law unto themselves: Which shew the work of the law written in their hearts, their conscience also bearing witness, and their thoughts the meanwhile accusing or else excusing one another.* (Romans 2:14,15 KJV)

The Jews of Paul's time argued that since the Gentiles did not have God's law, they were not as good as the Jews. They taught the law to the pagan Gentiles and told them how to obey God. These Jews thought themselves to be very righteous and holy. Like many Christians, they thought they were better than most.

Paul said that neither of them—Jews nor Gentiles—were good. For God demands absolute perfection, never turning back, never wavering, with "patient continuance in well doing." "We can't do it," Paul says. It's an impossible possibility.

JUDGMENT DAY

If we think God loves us because we've measured up, because we've done the deeds of the law, then we had better watch out. A day is coming when we will stand before God, and He will judge all of our secrets. *"In the day when God shall judge the secrets of men by Jesus Christ according to my Gospel"* (Romans 2:16).

Paul is saying that on the day we stand before God, those who have sought to follow God's law in order to have a right standing with God will be judged. The standard by which God judges us is Jesus Christ. If we try to present our case to God and say, "God, look at all I've done," God will gently say, "Come here. Compare yourself to my Son. This is my Son in whom I am well pleased. How do you measure up?"

You know what we will do? Paul says we will *"accuse or else excuse one another"* (Romans 2:15b). We will accuse others and then start excusing ourselves. We will say, "Wait a minute, God, why are you drawing the spotlight on me? Look at Joe over there; look at Susie. What about them?"

THE BIG SURPRISE

On that day, many who stand before God will be surprised. You may be one of them. If you are trying to follow the Law to obtain your approval from God, it may be that you have never been changed by the grace of God. You may be unregenerate. You may not be saved.

You may be unregenerate because the natural man, like the Gentiles of Paul's day, attempts to follow some type of law to measure up, even if it is just his own conscience. Only by a work of grace can the natural man see the impossibility of trying to measure up. Only the Gospel slays self.

There will be those who stand before God and think they've just really done a pretty fine job. But God will say to them, *"Depart from me ye who work iniquity"* (Matthew 7:23b). They will be shocked and surprised.

It's like the man who went to a store to buy a gift for his wife. He said to the salesman, "Sir, I would like to buy my wife some gloves."

The salesman said, "Is this a surprise to her?"

He replied, "Yes, she's expecting a mink coat."

There are a lot of people who will stand before God expecting a "mink coat," and they are not going to get it. They are expecting God's acceptance because of their personal holiness. What they don't understand is that God demands perfection. It is impossible for us to be perfect.

JESUS DID THE IMPOSSIBLE

However, there was One who performed the Law—every jot and tittle, in thought, action, and deed. Within Him was no guile. He was born of a virgin, without a sin nature. He was the perfect man. He is the only one who lived his life the way we were intended to live it. He accomplished the impossible. What a wonderful thought!

Yet he died a sinner's death. He didn't deserve it.

Why did He die? He died as our substitute. He died the death due every one of us who violated the law of God just once.

Through His Son, God did for us what the Law couldn't do. When Jesus Christ died, all of the condemnation and the death due us because of our violation of the Law was placed upon Jesus Christ. His death is

> ❧
> *We are clothed in Christ's righteousness. Since He is holy, we are holy.*
> ❧

our pardon—His life is our holiness. His righteousness is given to those who believe; our sins are given to Him who died.

Christ will stand beside believers on the Day of Judgment. Even though we might be the chief of sinners, we will come before our Father without condemnation because Jesus fulfilled the law in our stead. We are clothed in His righteousness. Since He is holy, we are holy.

Instead of trying to do the impossible by measuring up to a standard, I am going to embrace the Son. I am going to love Jesus Christ. I am going to have a love relationship with the only person who ever fulfilled the law. He did the impossible. He is my holiness. I am perfect in Him.

SALVATION IS OF THE LORD

The following quotation by C. H. Spurgeon would put most churches out of business because they don't understand it:

> Salvation is a work of God. It is He alone who quickens the soul "dead in trespasses and sins," and it is He also who maintains the soul in its spiritual life . . . if I hold on in a consistent life, it is because He upholds me with His hand. . . . Whatever I have, all my goodness is of the Lord alone. Wherein I sin, that is my own; but wherein I act rightly, that is of God, wholly and completely. . . . Do I live before men a holy life? It is not I, but Christ who lives in me. . . . I am by *God's* chastisements sanctified to my good. . . . I find in God all that I want; but I find in myself nothing but sin and misery . . . without Jesus I can do nothing. . . . What Jonah learned in the great deep, let me learn this morning in my closet: "*Salvation is of the Lord*."

Most churches usually teach that salvation is what we do, how we act, and what we haven't done. They teach shame, judgment, and condemnation. I want to help you realize that true Christianity is falling in love with Jesus Christ.

OUR HOLINESS IN CHRIST

Paul taught that we *are* holy. He called the believers "saints" (the Greek word is *hagios* which means *holy*) in his letters to the early churches in the cities of Ephesus, Rome, Philippi, Colosse, and Corinth. Considering the problems in each of these churches, it was obvious he did not call them saints due to their own adherence to the law. They knew that it was solely the work of Christ that made them holy.

Although he called them saints, he was not blind to their problems. In the church at Corinth, an elder was living in adultery, the church was splitting four ways, and folks were getting drunk at the Lord's Supper. In fact, Paul wrote his letter to them to deal with these problems. But he began by telling the believers who and what they were. *"To the church of God which is at Corinth, to them that are ...called to be saints"* (I Corinthians 1:2).

Doesn't it seem dangerous to call the members of that dysfunctional church holy? Peter Lord in his book *Eagles and Turkeys* says:

> Who is going to be more careful not to get dirty, the man who believes his clothes are already filthy, or the man who is dressed in a white suit and feels like a million dollars? Why, of course, the man dressed in a white suit is going to be very careful not to stain it. And if he does get a stain on his suit, he will seek to remove it immediately. On the other hand, what possible difference does it make if you get one more spot on your filthy old dungarees?. . .
>
> The Christian life is not one where you climb uphill against great odds, to someday become holy. When you became his child, God placed you in His holiness. Your challenge is to know who you are in Christ.[1]

Your Father and Jesus Christ have said you are holy. Will you believe them, receive the gift of righteousness, and say, "I am holy"? In Christ, you *are* holy.

THE FREEDOM OF HOLINESS

Dan Heath, the worship leader in our church, was in prison one time. Excuse me—he was *visiting* a prison one time conducting a revival service. He asked for song requests. One of the prisoners requested the old, great hymn, "*Free From the Law, O Happy Condition.*" How appropriate.

We also should sing that hymn. We are "free from the law, O happy condition." Any church that puts us back under the law has lost sight of the Gospel of Jesus Christ.

By the way, when Dan asked the other prisoners if that was their favorite hymn, one man piped up and said, "No, my favorite hymn is *I'll Fly Away.*"

Some of you are captives to the futile effort of trying to keep the law. You have struggled with religion. You have tried, and tried, and tried to mortify the flesh. You have made every promise in the book. You have recommitted, rededicated, walked the aisle five, six, seven, eight, nine, ten times. You've been baptized two or three times. You are struggling against these bonds because you are trying to do the impossible. You are trying to make yourself holy.

The freedom of holiness does not mean that our life doesn't change. It means that we are not so much concerned about the exterior things that people do. We are free to just love people and be gracious to them. Grace becomes more than merely a word or a song that we sing. It's the way we live.

I AM HOLY

I know myself to be the chief of sinners, but I have a holiness that is apart from my obedience to the law. I have the holiness and righteousness of my Savior. It is mine, free of charge, by simple faith and trust.

I have discovered that when we realize who we are in Christ, then we don't have to be controlled by shame or manipulated by guilt. We don't have to be told what we should or shouldn't do. We want to serve God.

My kids once asked, "Dad, if you weren't a preacher, would we be going to church?" Yes, we would.

You know why we'd be going to church? We'd be going to church because we want to go to church. If I ever went to a church where a preacher tried to make me feel guilty for not being in church, I might not go to that church. The reason I'm at church is because God has done a work within me.

This is the paradox—the impossible possibility. Even though we cannot ever achieve holiness by our performance, God says we are holy. We *are* saints. For His elect it is no longer an impossibility, it is a fact—we are holy.

We are holy because Jesus Christ is holy, and we are clothed in *His* righteousness. By God's grace we are as we ought to be—perfect in Christ.

Oh, to be accepted
in a feeling sort of way:
to be known for what I am—
not what I do or say.

Charles Solomon

Chapter 13
I Am Accepted

He hath made us accepted in the beloved.
Ephesians 1:6b (KJV)

I have one or two cantankerous people in my church. They come to business meetings with chips on their shoulders, they fire off emails to me when they don't like what I say, and they make life miserable for their Sunday School teachers and co-workers.

My human nature does not want to accept these cranky critics. I want to avoid them, write them off, and hope they don't darken my door.

But I have found if I accept them, if I hear them out, if I don't try to argue with them, that often they become effective and involved. Once they find they are accepted, their crankiness and irritability are softened. Once they find out they are free to express themselves without negative feedback, there is a change in their spirit. They begin to lose their bitterness and become more accepting of others.

And why shouldn't I accept them? God accepted me in Christ.

GOD WILL NEVER, NEVER, NEVER, NEVER, NEVER FORSAKE US

In the original Greek, the following verse has five negatives: *"For He hath said, I will never leave thee, nor forsake thee"* (Hebrews 13:5b KJV).

In Greek *ou* and *em* are both forms of the word *not*. They are sometimes translated as *by no means*. So the verse is, "For He Himself has said, *ou em* (or *not, not*) shall I desert you nor *ou em* (or *not, not*) shall I forsake you." (The fifth negative is *nor*.)

Paul says, "I (that is the Lord) will not leave you; no, I will not, I will not, I will not, I will not forsake you." In using five negatives, he emphasizes how important it is for believers to know that God will *never* forsake or reject us— will *never* abandon us.

OVERT AND COVERT REJECTION

Why do we have trouble grasping the fact that we are accepted by God? Why did Paul think he had to emphasize it five times? It is because we all have had periods of unhappiness due to rejection from others. Rejection is the opposite of acceptance. We transfer our hurts and these feelings of rejection from others to our relationship with God.

Overt rejection is open or obvious and sometimes aggressive. It conveys the message that one is unwanted or unloved.

Any child who is physically, sexually, emotionally, or spiritually abused by his or her parents is receiving overt, aggressive rejection. Any child who has a parent who says, "I hate you," or, "I wish you'd never been born," or words similar to that is receiving overt rejection from his or her parent.

As an adult, if you have a spouse who abandons you, who is unfaithful, who has an affair, or marries someone else, you experience this kind of rejection—this overt, open rejection. It is extremely crushing to be overtly rejected because we feel undesirable and outcast.

Covert rejection is not as obvious. It is subtle.

This rejection is felt when someone doesn't necessarily say, "I hate you," but puts conditions upon acceptance of others. He or she might say something like, "You know, I love you when . . . ," or "I love you if . . ."

It could be more negative, showing disappointment. It might not be an outright "I hate you," but something like, "You are disappointing to me."

Covert rejection can take place in the life of a child when the parent is a workaholic. This parent has no idea he is communicating to that child "I reject you." Frankly, the message the child receives is, "You don't love me. You don't want to spend time with me. You're never here. You're never with me." It is not intended, but that is the message that is received. If a child grows up perceiving that a parent doesn't want to spend time with him or her, this is covert rejection. This covert, unintentional rejection communicated by the workaholic also affects the marriage relationship.

The Results of Rejection

When we experience rejection in our lives, our emotions are greatly affected. We will have the tendency to do one of two things:

We will withdraw and never allow ourselves to be emotionally attached to an individual because we've been hurt by someone close to us.

Or we will become fakes. We can't be real because we are afraid that if we show who we really are, then people will reject us. So we put on a front. We can't say what we feel because we're afraid of rejection. We say what we believe to be the appropriate thing.

It happens in the subtlest of ways. We can't even ask someone to do something for us because if they say, "No," we take that as rejection.

We live a life of manipulation and control, hiding behind a persona that's really not ourselves. It would scare us to death to really unzip our soul and let people see who we are because we fear rejection.

GOD ACCEPTS US

When we experience rejection in a human relationship, it carries over into our relationship with God.

God is a spirit. We worship Him in spirit and in truth. Because He is a spirit, He transcends us. We would never know God unless He condescended and came down to our level because He is so much higher than we are. But God is gracious, and He has condescended and shown us who He is through His Son, the Living Word, and the Bible, the written word.

We transfer feelings of rejection from others to our relationship with God

God's Son, Jesus Christ, took upon Himself the form of a servant. He humbled Himself, came to earth as a man, and became obedient to death on the cross (Philippians 2:5-8).

He did that so we could be accepted. And we *are* accepted, but not by anything we do, *"For it is God who works in you both to will and to do of His good pleasure"* (Philippians 2:13).

BUT I DON'T FEEL IT

Many come to me saying, "I understand what you're saying. I have it up here, right here in my mind. I know the truth that God loves me. I know the Bible says God loves me unconditionally. But why, in my heart, do I have a hard time believing it? Why don't I feel it? Why do I feel like God is angry with me, that He is punishing and rejecting me? Why do I feel that way? I have it in my mind, but I can't get it down to my heart."

My reply to them is "It may be because you've had very few experiences in relationships in this world where you've been loved unconditionally on an emotional level—maybe none at all."

Our relationship with God is a spiritual relationship, which rightly should involve the emotions. But our human emotions might not let us feel that God accepts us, and loves us, and will not reject us, unless, by the grace of God, we have experienced a relationship on earth where we have felt acceptance.

Some reading this book might say, "You are right, I've never really had a relationship where I felt like I have been accepted unconditionally. Can I get to the place where I believe God accepts me that way?"

> *Our human emotions might not let us feel that God accepts us.*

Yes, you can—by a work of the Spirit.

It can happen, but don't be surprised or discouraged if you have to work through a tremendous amount of difficulties. By the grace of God, as you study the word, fellowship with believers, and communicate with your Father, you can come to the place where you can feel the love of God.

I believe this can happen because I have heard the testimonies of many who have moved into an awareness of God's acceptance.

But remember what you have been reading in this book. We are not accepted because of what we do. We are accepted because of what Christ has done for us.

SYMPTOMS OF REJECTION

Even though it might be difficult for us to lay down our defenses and trust in God's acceptance of us, we should begin the process. Because if we can't come to the place where we feel the acceptance of God, then we are continually going to have difficulties in our relationship with God, ourselves, and others.

We will have a sense of worthlessness. We will feel so unworthy that we will constantly batter ourselves and beat ourselves to death. We think God is angry because we feel as if we don't measure up or meet His standard. (Often we cover up feelings of worthlessness with an air of superiority.)

We will say, "I know I'm not the way I'm supposed to be. This year I'm gonna do all I can to be better." We'll make vows to attend church more, to do more for God. We'll make promises to pray and to read the Bible. We'll make all kinds of performance-related resolutions.

Those are good things, and we should aspire to do all of them. But our motivation is not to get God to think more highly of us. We're already accepted in the Beloved One. He will give us the grace to feel that acceptance.

Feelings of escape are indications we have no idea that God accepts us and will not reject us. If we don't feel God's acceptance, we will wish we were someone else or that we just weren't here. We might think, "If I could just arrange things so that my children were taken care of, so that everything would run smoothly without me here, I'd just disappear."

A church member once said to me, "It's not that I want to commit suicide. That's not it at all. I know that's wrong. In fact, I'm a chicken. It's just that I fantasize about being gone. I just wish I was outta here."

Depression is often unresolved anger. Depressed people turn their anger within and don't express it because they are afraid if they did, they would be rejected by God and others, so they turn it within. This inner anger causes them to become bitter, and depression sets in. They sometimes need the help of a professional counselor to help them find the root of those feelings of rejection that have built up in them.

We will withdraw if we feel rejected by God and by others. We will hide behind walls to keep others out. But not only are we protecting ourselves from the rejection of others, we are preventing others from knowing us.

> ❧
> *We are already accepted*
> *in the Beloved One.*
> ❧

Our fear of rejection will make us think we must be what others expect us to be. We won't unwind, relax, or just be ourselves. We will not let ourselves show emotion. We'll not let people see weakness in us.

Perfectionism is an indication of a struggle with rejection. A perfectionist is obsessed with feelings of failure if they haven't gotten everything just right—dotted every *i*, crossed every *t*, got the margins just perfect, polished the car, washed the cat.

They believe their acceptance is based upon performance. So everything has to be perfect for them to feel comfortable and accepted. A perfectionist believes, "If I can just do everything perfectly, I will be loved and accepted."

Anxiety is nothing but the fear of rejection. What are you afraid of? Are you afraid of rejection by your spouse, your boss, your co-workers?

If, as a believer, we feel anxiety about death, what are we afraid of? Are we afraid God will reject us?

Do we have anxiety about tomorrow? God accepts us and cares about us. He who feeds the fowls of the air and arrays the lilies of the field knows what we need and will provide for us. We can rest in His acceptance and *"take no thought for tomorrow; for tomorrow shall take thought for the things of itself"* (Matthew 6:34).

We will either *bring* guilt or *bear* guilt if we feel God rejects us.

We will *bring guilt* to those around us by what we say and what we expect of them. We will be critical and try to make them tow the line. If we feel that God expects us to be perfect, we will expect others to be perfect. Sadly, the only ones we will succeed in bringing guilt to are the weak, those others who don't feel the acceptance of God.

Or, we will *bear guilt*. We will always feel guilty. But this kind of guilt doesn't lead to the cross to receive forgiveness and acceptance in the Beloved. This guilt just hangs like a dead weight dragging us down into bitterness and despondency.

OUR RELATIONSHIPS

Until we are able to understand that, as believers, we are unconditionally accepted by God, the emotions connected with rejection can destroy us. The pride will poison our relationships with God and others.

We won't enjoy life. We won't enjoy our spouses or our kids but will just tolerate them. They may feel that we love them based on what they can give us.

We will manipulate others to try to get our happiness from them because we are not getting our happiness from God when we feel rejected (and think we ought to be accepted).

> ❧
> *The emotions connected*
> *with rejection*
> *can destroy us.*
> ❧

We will resent God and be angry with Him. How could God allow this to happen to *me*? How could He bring this to *my* life? Why does God seem to give *me* the toughest problems?

SELF-CENTEREDNESS

Lest you think I feel sorry for those who have feelings of rejection, hang onto your hats, because I'm going to tell you the root of feelings of rejection—the root of the problem is a self-centered life.

Feelings of rejection are nothing but a symptom of the sin called self-centeredness. If we are struggling with rejection, our biggest struggle is pride because we want desperately to be accepted, and, down deep, we feel like we really ought to be accepted.

When we feel that we are not accepted, we cover up our feelings of worthlessness, find forms of escapism, withdraw, become obsessed with perfectionism, get anxious, get depressed, and bear or bring guilt. We feel all of this because we are too proud to get ourselves off the throne of our lives and rest in the fact that, in Christ, *"I am accepted."*

If we see ourselves showing symptoms of rejection, we need to know that we can never do anything to get God to accept us more. We are accepted because He has chosen to accept us.

WE ARE ACCEPTED IN THE SON

When we can come to the understanding, in spiritual language, that we are big, fat sinners; but God, in His mercy, has chosen to save sinners like us; when we trust that He has chosen to save us through His Son, rather than through our works; then we can rest in the acceptance found in the Beloved One. We can, by faith, accept the truth that God accepts us because of His Son.

We can rest in Him and claim the promise of Paul in Hebrews 13:5 that He will not, He will not, He will not, He will not, He will not forsake us. Not because of who we are, but because of who His Son is.

We are displaying pride if we constantly beat ourselves up because we are not what we believe God would have us be, or what we think we ought to be. Pride is what causes us to think we can become what God wants us to become by trying harder, shaping up, and doing more. We are not seeing that our acceptance is in the Son.

You might say, "But, as believers, don't we try to serve God and love God? Don't we try to do things for God?" Of course we do! Absolutely! I want to go to the grave working my fingers to the bone for the Lord Jesus.

But why do we serve Him? We do it because we love Him, rather than striving to gain acceptance.

TAKE THE CURE

For us to be whole, we must trust in God's unconditional acceptance of us. We must do it for our own happiness, as well as the happiness of those around us. Until we understand God's acceptance, we will not be able to accept others unconditionally.

The fellowship of the church, the body of Christ, suffers when there is no spirit of acceptance. The church becomes exclusive and intolerant. Members are backbiting, bitter, and faultfinding. In his song, "If This Is Not a Place," Ken Medema says:

> *If this is not a place where tears are understood,*
> *where can I go to cry?*
> *And if this is not a place where my spirit can take wing,*
> *where can I go to fly?*
> *And if this is not a place where my questions can be asked,*
> *where shall I go to seek?*
> *And if this is not a place where my heart cries can be heard,*
> *where can I go to speak?*
> *I don't need another place for trying to impress you*
> *with just how good and virtuous I am.*
> *I don't need another place for always being on top of things;*
> *everybody knows that it's a sham.*
> *I don't need another place for always wearing smiles,*
> *even when it's not the way I feel.*
> *I don't need another place to mouth*
> *the same old platitudes;*
> *Cause you and I both know that it's not real.*
> *If this is not a place where tears are understood,*
> *where shall I go? Where can I go to cry?*

Once we realize that we are accepted, then we are free to accept others. The church can then become what it was meant to be—a place of acceptance and grace.

IT COULD BE WORSE

If you are still struggling with acceptance because you are looking at your circumstances and, frankly, things look tough, then let me remind you of King David. We think we have it tough? Our problems do not begin to compare with his.

David, the great king of Israel, the anointed of God, the sweet psalmist of Israel, had a dysfunctional family. At least one of his wives despised him. His kids were in rebellion. One of his sons wanted to kill him in order to get the throne.

Think of the overwhelming rejection. But David said, *"Although my house be not so with God* [what that means is, that everything in my house is not the way it should be, ought to be, or the way I'd even want it to be], *yet He has made with me an everlasting covenant, ordered in all things, and sure"* (II Samuel 23:5).

WE ARE ACCEPTED

David knew that, despite his circumstances, he got his happiness from the covenant God made with him. If we are believers, God has established a covenant of unconditional love with us. Though it may be tough for us in this life, we are to get our happiness from what God has said to us, "You are accepted. You will never be rejected."

> *God will not, will not, will not, will not, will not forsake us.*

There is a beautiful poem by Charles Solomon that goes like this:

> *Oh, to know acceptance*
> *   in a feeling sort of way:*
> *To be known for what I am—*
> *   not what I do or say.*
> *It's nice to be loved and wanted*
> *   for the person I seem to be,*
> *But my heart cries out to be loved*
> *   for the person who is really me.*
>
> *To be able to drop all the fronts and*
> *   share with another my fears,*
> *Would bring such relief to my soul,*
> *   though accompanied by many tears.*
> *When I find this can be done*
> *   without the pain of rejection,*
> *   then will my joy be complete.*
> *And feelings toward self know correction.*
>
> *The path to feeling acceptance of God*
> *   is paved with acceptance on earth;*
> *Being valued by others I love*
> *   enhances my own feeling of worth.*
> *Oh, the release and freedom He gives*
> *   as I behold His wonderful face—*
> *As Jesus makes real my acceptance in Him,*
> *   and I learn the true meaning of grace.*
>
> *A pity it is that so late we find*
> *   His love need not be earned;*
> *As we yield to Him all manner of strife*
> *   a precious truth has been learned.*
> *Then, as we share with others who search*
> *   for love and acceptance and rest;*
> *They'll find in us the Savior's love*
> *   and experience the end of their quest.*

*Jesus wills for us to have
our hearts primarily in heaven,
our hopes primarily in heaven,
our longings primarily in heaven,
our joy primarily in heaven.*

John Piper

Chapter 14
I Am Rewarded

And, behold, I come quickly;
and my reward is with me, to give every man
according as his work will be.
Revelation 22:12 (KJV)

In his book, *The Summons*, John Grisham writes of an old judge who issued a summons for his two sons to come home because he was dying and wanted to talk to them about the administration of his estate.

One son got there before the other and found that his father had already died. In looking around the house, he found three and a half million dollars worth of cash in some cabinets behind a sofa. The book deals with how this cash changed the son's life for the worse.

It was a sad book to read. It was sad to read how destructive the possessions were to that son. Finally, he realized that the money was not so important to him. At the end, we find him and his brother dealing with their difficult relationship and discovering how the money has affected both of them.

That is the way our world turns. Many become so focused on material possessions that they lose sight of relationships.

As believers, we are children of God and joint-heirs with Christ (Romans 8:17). This special relationship with God brings special rewards. But sometimes we don't realize that more important than the blessings God gives to us is the blessing of our relationship with God, the Father, Himself.

THE SUBJECT OF REWARDS

In researching the subject of rewards for this book, I find myself in the same position as A. W. Pink. He said "the subject of *rewards* is a wide one" and was, therefore, only able to deal with it briefly in his article, "The Examination and Rewarding of the Believer's Works." There is much more about rewards than I, too, will be able to cover in this one chapter.

Rewards are often mentioned in the Bible but, quite frankly, have been the subject of debate for centuries. Not only do I feel limited to cover the wide scope of the subject of rewards, but I also feel limited to cover the extent of the debate. Here are just a few verses concerning rewards:

"Rejoice, and be exceeding glad: for great is your reward in heaven: for so persecuted they the prophets which were before you" (Matthew 5:12).

"Take heed that you do not your alms before men, to be seen of them: otherwise you have no reward of your Father which is in heaven" (Matthew 6:1).

"Knowing that of the Lord you shall receive the reward of the inheritance: for you serve the Lord Christ" (Colossians 3:24).

"That they should be judged, and that you should give reward to your servants the prophets, and to the saints, and them that fear your name, small and great" (Revelation 11:18).

"And, behold I come quickly; and my reward is with me, to give every man according as his work will be" (Revelation 22:12).

If you have been paying attention while reading this book, you should have begun to realize that the idea of a
Christian being rewarded for merit is the opposite of what the book has been about. A reward is something given for good deeds, service, or merit. It carries with it

> &
> *Grace is unmerited favor;*
> *but reward based on*
> *works would be merited.*
> &

the idea of wages, of that which can be earned. So how can this be? How can a believer "earn" rewards?

The New Testament speaks clearly against obtaining salvation as a reward, or wages, for work done. Grace means *unmerited* favor, and reward based on works is *merited*. By contrast, the Bible declares that *"the wages of sin is death, but the gift of God is eternal life in Christ Jesus our Lord"* (Romans 6:23). Only wages can be worked for—not gifts.

If our righteousness is in Christ, if all the work has already been done by Him to secure our salvation, then how can we add anything to His work by our performance?

OUR IDEAS OF REWARDS

Most of us who are believers have probably heard about rewards for a Christian, both here on earth and in heaven. We hear things like: "Look at Aunt Bessie over there. She will certainly have a lot of stars in her crown when she gets to heaven." (As opposed to Uncle Bill who we think will be lucky to get in.) Or we think we need to work hard if we want to live in a mansion in the more upscale regions of heaven, rather than a mud hut in the slums.

There is a Christian culture that is focused on what God can give us. Christian books tell us how to pray to bring favor and blessing from God. They say that our eternal rewards will be based upon our making the right decisions today.

On the other hand, so-called "enlightened" believers dismiss the idea of rewards as selfish. In this case, self-denial becomes an end in itself. They believe that to desire our own good and earnestly hope for the enjoyment of it is a bad thing. John Piper says this notion has crept in from Kant and the Stoics and is no part of the Christian faith. He believes our desire for glory and honor and immortality is not too strong but too weak:

> Jesus wills for us to have our hearts primarily in heaven, our hopes primarily in heaven, our longings primarily in heaven, our joy primarily in heaven. There is no other way that you can rejoice and be glad at the loss of your earthly joys. How shall we rejoice and be glad when these things are taken from us if we have not loved heaven more?[1]

THE WEIGHT OF GLORY

In his essay, "The Weight of Glory," C. S. Lewis says our glory will be when we stand before our Maker, and He says to us, "Well done, thou good and faithful servant." Many of us resist the idea of being patted on the back, but Lewis says proud misunderstanding is behind the dislike of being patted on the back. The humblest, most childlike of pleasures, in its purest form, is the desire to please those whom we love and respect:

> To please God . . . to be a real ingredient in the divine happiness . . . to be loved by God, not merely pitied, but delighted in as an artist delights in his work or a father in a son—it seems impossible, a weight or burden of glory which our thoughts can hardly sustain. But so it is.[2]

Of all the promises found in Scripture, Lewis says nothing, no kind of reward that we can ever imagine, compares with the idea that for eternity we shall be with Christ.[3]

FALSE TEACHING ON REWARDS

A false understanding of rewards promotes pride. Some of our ideas about rewards are nothing more than self-righteous pride. As Don Fortner says:

> If one person could obtain a bigger crown, a higher rank, or a greater nearness to God by his works than another, he would have every reason to pop his suspenders, strut around heaven, and have those poor, crownless people, living in the back street slums of the New Jerusalem, bow and scrape before him.[4]

A false understanding of rewards is based upon works. We believe we can do something that will put God in obligation to us. We pray that certain prayer, or we work and work, so that God will owe us that bigger mansion or that extra star. *"Now to him that works is the reward not reckoned of grace, but of debt"* (Romans 4:4).

When we work for something, what we are paid is not *grace*—it is what we are owed. It is a debt. If my works made me right with God, then my life would not be a life of grace.

When I was a teenager, I had a little business called "Quality Lawn Care." I would mow a yard, rake it, and edge it. When I finished, I would knock on the door of the house; and when the owner came to the door, I would say, "I have finished my work. I am ready to be paid." She would write out a check or give me cash.

If my employer had withheld the money owed me after I had done the work, I would have been very upset because I did not consider my payment to be a payment of grace. It was a debt owed to me.

We carry this same thinking over into our rewards from God. When we believe that we must work really hard to be rewarded by God and formulate a list in our minds of things to do in order to obtain His favor, then we put God in debt to us. If we could work for the favor of God, then our life would not be a life of grace. It would be a life of debt.

It is impossible for us to work to obtain God's favor. It is impossible for God to ever like us, or accept us, or bless us, or reward us, or favor us because of anything we do. If that were the case, He would owe us.

If we believe God owes us, then when the storms come, we'll get angry and bitter and argue with God, "Why, God? Why? Why me? Look at all I've done for you! Why am I sick? Why has my wife left? Why have I lost my job? Why has this happened to me? Look at all I've done."

You are a sinner, and I am a sinner. *"For all have sinned, and come short of the glory of God"* (Romans 3:23). God owes us nothing. But He has chosen to be gracious to sinners, abundantly gracious. Whatever it is that we receive, whether it's a breath, a dollar—not even to mention a home, a family —whatever it is that we get, we don't deserve it. It is all of grace, and we should be extremely grateful.

Our works are filthy rags. If we think we are going to stand before God and try to convince Him that we should be rewarded for our self-generated list of good works, we need to remember that all of our works are done with the taint of sin. Even Aunt Bessie's years of loyal service are just filthy rags in the sight of the infinitely holy Lord God.

We may be surprised to find that our proudest accomplishments, the works that we thought were most going to make the cut, will be burned like the stubble of the field (I Corinthians 3:11-15). Our works will be judged by the divine standard. According to A. W. Pink, the works which have issued from the divine nature within us will receive reward, "but those which were wrought by those who felt they must do something, those performed in the energy of the flesh, those done merely for self-aggrandizement will all be burned up."

We would feel shame when we got to heaven if we had to do certain things to receive our rewards. If we believe we have not done enough to earn our rewards, then we must also believe that we might feel ashamed of ourselves when we get to heaven. We might be embarrassed by our small crown (or even lack of one) and might feel envy at Aunt Bessie's diamond-studded tiara. If we were going to feel shame in heaven, that would make it a place of sorrow. But we know it will be a place of everlasting bliss.

Our salvation is not limited. As believers, we will not have to deal with the issue of sin. Some will be surprised to find that their sins will not be counted against them when they get to heaven. For believers, the sin question has been closed forever. Our sins were all judged

> ✂
> *Nothing . . . compares with the idea that for eternity we shall be with Christ.*
> ✂

at the cross where Jesus Christ, our Substitute, died. Jesus has done *all* the work needed for our salvation. But His work was not limited to just our salvation. He has also done *all* the work for our righteousness.

C. S. Lewis describes "what might happen when the redeemed soul, beyond all hope and nearly beyond belief, learns at last that she has pleased Him whom she was created to please." There will be no room for vanity then. She will be free from the miserable illusion that is her doing. He goes on:

> It is written that we shall "stand before" Him, shall appear, shall be inspected. The promise of glory is the promise, almost incredible and only possible by the work of Christ, that some of us, that any of us who really chooses, shall actually survive that examination, shall find approval, shall please God.[5]

Materialism enters into our doctrine of rewards. When we focus on earning material rewards, we are usually carrying baggage from our earthly perspectives into heaven. Crowns, mansions, and cottages are earthly, material possessions.

We often speak of these temporal rewards in terms of "health and wealth." We judge God's favor to others by how He has rewarded them with success, prosperity, and healing of all their diseases. This is just another manifestation of the "prosperity gospel." The "prosperity gospel" looks for the gifts rather than the Giver. It promises what God can give us, rather than God Himself.

All the rewards we think we might want pale in comparison to the Almighty God. All the crowns, the thrones, the mansions, the status we are hoping for will be nothing when we are in the presence of God Himself.

Our greatest hope of reward is the very presence of the all-wise, omnipotent, gracious, loving God. We inherit Him for all eternity. Heaven will be heaven because God is there. He is our reward.

Suffering is one of the most precious of our rewards,
but it would not be high on our list of perks for being a
Christian. We are looking for tangible, material rewards.
However, I have come to believe that suffering is the threshold into the presence of God Himself.

During my ministry, I have been at the side of countless
believers who have endured almost unbearable suffering. I
have often observed that those times of suffering have drawn
them closer to God than they have ever been.

Could not our Father prevent the suffering? If He
delights in us, can't He keep us
from suffering? Let me ask you,
"Could God have saved you
apart from the suffering and
death of Jesus Christ? No!"

*Could God have saved you
apart from the suffering
and death of Jesus Christ?*

As joint heirs we will share grace and glory with our
Savior Jesus Christ. We will be "glorified together" in heaven.
That is our ultimate reward. But we are also heirs to His
suffering. We are: *"heirs of God, and joint heirs with Christ; if so
be that we suffer with him, that we may be also glorified together"*
(Romans 8:17). Jesus told His disciples, *"In this world, you
shall have tribulation but be of good cheer"* (John 16:33).

So for the time that we are on this earth *"the whole creation groans and travails in pain"* (Romans 8:22). But as we
suffer, we suffer with the Son. Suffering is not a sign of God's
disapproval. It is a sign that we are joint heirs with His Son.

We expect God to be fair in His rewards. It would not
be fair for Uncle Bill to receive as great a reward in heaven as
Aunt Bessie. After all, she worked and worked for Jesus all
her life. She taught Sunday School, Vacation Bible School,

sang in the choir, and on and on. But Uncle Bill didn't even become a believer until his later years.

When we enter eternity, we may be surprised to see Uncle Bill with the exact rewards as Aunt Bessie. If we were still in our earthly mindset, we, along with Aunt Bessie, might cry out, "It isn't fair! She did so much. She served for so many years, yet here comes Uncle Bill by the skin of his teeth and gets the same reward as she does. It just doesn't seem fair for God to do that."

I decided to take one of my children golfing in celebration of his birthday—just the two of us. One of my other children complained, "Dad, it's just not fair." I said, "What do you mean?" My child replied, "It's not fair that Kade gets to go by himself with you."

Modern man is married to the concept of fairness. We believe that everyone desires equal treatment. Everyone wants to be treated fairly. All we have to do is look at the vocabulary of business or government: equal employment, equal rights, equal access. Fairness, to most, means that everyone is treated the same.

> &
> *Would it surprise you to learn that the Bible never calls God fair?*
> &

Would it surprise you to learn that *the Bible never calls God fair?*

THE LORD OF THE VINEYARD

Jesus told a parable that clearly illustrates the fairness of God. Peter had just asked the Lord what reward he would get for giving up all and following Jesus. Jesus told Peter what was in store for him in heaven. He surprised him by saying that in heaven *"many who are first will be last, and many who are last will be first"* (Matthew 19:30). Then He told this parable:

> *For the kingdom of heaven is like a man that is a house-holder; which went out early in the morning to hire laborers into his vineyard. When he had agreed with the laborers for a penny a day, he sent them into his vineyard.*
>
> *And he* [the landowner, or the lord of the vineyard], *went out about the third hour and saw others standing idle in the market place, and said to them; "Go also into the vineyard and whatever is right I will give you." And they went their way.*
>
> *Again he went out about the sixth and ninth hour, and did likewise. And about the eleventh hour he went out, and found others standing idle, and said to them, "Why stand you here all the day idle?"*
>
> *They said to him, "Because no man has hired us."*
>
> *He said to them, "Go also into the vineyard. Whatever is right, that shall you receive."*
>
> *So when evening came the Lord of the vineyard said to his steward, "Call the laborers and give them their hire, beginning from the last* [that is he who was hired at the eleventh hour] *unto the first* [that is those who were hired at the beginning of the day].*"*
>
> *When they came that were hired about the eleventh hour, they received every man a penny* [a day's wages]. *But when the first came, they supposed that they should have received more; and they likewise received every man a penny* [a day's wages]. *When they had received it, they murmured against the goodman of the house, saying, "These that were hired last have worked but one hour, and you have made them equal to us, which have borne the burden and the heat of the day."*
>
> *But he answered one of them and said, "Friend, I do you no wrong, did not you agree with me for a penny? Take what yours is, and go your way: I will give to this last, even as to you. Is it not lawful for me to do what I will with my own? Is your eye evil, because I am good?"*
>
> *So the last shall be first, and the first shall be last: for many be called but few chosen.* (Matthew 20:1-16)

THE CHARACTER OF THE LORD OF THE VINEYARD

The Lord of the vineyard represents Jesus Himself. In the parable, He said to one of the grumblers, *"Friend, I do you no wrong"* (Matthew 20:13a). This means that He never does anyone wrong, for he is a just (or fair) Lord. Jesus Christ Himself is said to be just in all of His ways, the King of saints.

He is just to the sinner. When the Bible says God is angry with the wicked every day, do not think that God is angry without cause.

If you are apart from Jesus Christ and saving faith in His death and blood, one of these days you will stand before the Judge of this universe. He will say to you, *"Depart from me, you who work iniquity"* (Matthew 7:23). You will wind up in hell because of your sins because a just God justly punishes sin. Rewards will not be an issue with you. Your life will be shown for what it is. You will have no complaint against a just, holy God because your nature and conduct is sinful in all its activity. God is just to the sinner.

> ☙
> *The Lord of the vineyard,*
> *Jesus Christ, Himself,*
> *is just in all of His ways.*
> ☙

He is just to the saint. The Bible tells us *"there is now no condemnation to them who are in Christ"* (Romans 8:1). How can it be that a just God can forgive a sinner like Wade Burleson? Does He forgive me by bypassing His justice? Absolutely not!

Jesus Christ was punished for my sin. The justice of God was satisfied when, on the cross, Christ endured the anger of God on behalf of Wade Burleson.

God is gracious. The Lord of the vineyard said, *"I will give to this one who was hired last just as I give to those of you who were hired first"* (Matthew 20:14).

Let's get the picture. The Lord of the vineyard goes out looking for people to work in the vineyard. He hires some individuals in the morning and agrees with them that He will pay them a day's wages. Throughout the day, He goes out and looks for workers—the third hour, the sixth hour, the ninth hour, the eleventh hour. Finally, after twelve hours, all of the workers are called in, and the Lord of the vineyard gives every one of them a day's wages.

Is it fair that the one who worked all day is paid the same amount as the one who worked for only an hour? Is it fair that the Lord of the vineyard gives more grace to one than He does another? No, it's not fair.

Why did He give the one called at the eleventh hour a day's wages? Because of His grace, because of His desire to give, and because it was His choice to do so. He was not obligated to do so, but by His grace He gave a day's wages.

THE COMPLAINT OF THE LABORERS

When the other workers saw this, they began to grumble, to complain, to murmur, saying under their breath, "I can't believe it. This one hired the eleventh hour has been paid the same amount as I. It's not fair. I should be paid more!"

Some of our thoughts may have been the thoughts of those who have worked in the vineyard all day. We have looked around and seen those who have more wealth or possessions, who have been more gifted, who have received more favor, who have been more graced. We think to ourselves, "But God, I have faithfully served you. I have dedicated my life to you. I have been in the vineyard all day. I have worked until I am tired. Lord, you owe me more!"

The workers complained because they supposed that they should have received more. They began to get a high opinion of their work. Pride entered into the equation. Ego—self—began to rear its ugly head.

When the Lord of the vineyard answered one of the grumblers, He said, "Friend, I do you no wrong." Isn't it good that God calls this grumbler "friend"? Isn't it good that He calls us His friends?

If God treated us according to the way we sometimes think, we would not be here today—but God is merciful. Even when we grumble against God, we still find the Lord Jesus saying, "*Friend*, I do you no wrong."

BY THE GRACE OF GOD

Wherever we are, at whatever station in life our train has come to rest, we are in the vineyard of God's kingdom by the grace of God. If we look around and see other people who seem to be rewarded with more, or more gifted, or talented, or have more ability, and begin to resent the fact that we are not what we think we ought to be; remember that we are in the vineyard of God's kingdom by His grace. We are where we are because of the grace of God. He is good to us. He has done us no wrong.

> *We are in the vineyard of God's kingdom by the grace of God.*

Don't think of yourself more highly than you ought. You are a preacher by the grace of God. You are a student by the grace of God. You are a teacher by the grace of God. You are a worker by the grace of God. In this parable, the Lord of the vineyard went out, and *He* called every one of the workers into the vineyard. The grace of the Lord is what brought the workers into the vineyard.

Has God Done Us Wrong?

We might look around and think that we deserve more. What do we deserve? We deserve death, hell, and condemnation. But, by the grace of God, He has rescued us.

We think, "I deserve to be rewarded, I deserve more in this life. I deserve more wealth. I deserve more prestige. I deserve more recognition." Why? God has done us no wrong.

We keep looking around at other people and comparing ourselves to them saying, "God, it's not fair!" The Bible never says life is fair nor that God is fair. The Bible says God is just, He is gracious, and He is merciful. Some have been given more grace. So be it. The grace that God has given to each one of us is sufficient.

The Lord of the vineyard doesn't treat everyone the same. He doesn't have to. He is Lord! He does no one wrong. The complaint of the workers, "God, I deserve better!" will destroy us. We don't deserve anything better. We must avoid that complaint. If we're angry, discontent, or unhappy, we don't know what it means to bow to the Lord of the vineyard.

The challenge to us is to be faithful, dedicated, devoted, workers in the vineyard. Wherever God has put you, keep on keeping on. Work the vineyard, plant the grapes, till the soil, pull the weeds, harvest the crop.

When it comes time for the day to end, we will all stand in the presence of a gracious Lord. We won't be complaining and comparing rewards. We will be in harmony with the Lord of the vineyard.

YOU AIN'T SEEN NOTHIN' YET!

Never forget where our hope lies. There is no comparison between this finite life, however great it may be, and the infinite.

Robert Haldane said, "If Moses' face shined on a mountain surrounded by the terrors of the testimonies of God's law, think about your face in heaven surrounded by the everlasting testimonies of His favor and blessing."

"For I reckon that the sufferings of this present time are not worthy to be compared with the glory which shall be revealed in us" (Romans 8:18).

I am rewarded, I have been rewarded, but my greatest hope lies in my final reward. And my final reward is the eternal bliss and joy of being in the presence of God.

Imagine yourself as a living house.
God comes in to rebuild that house. . . .

You thought you were going to be
made into a decent little cottage:
but He is building a palace.
He intends to come and
live in it Himself.

C. S. Lewis

Chapter 15
I Am His

For we are His workmanship . . .
Ephesians 2:10a

This book is *my* workmanship. Some time ago I chose to write it. I created it. I have formed it. I hope it is my masterpiece. I hope it will change your life.

I am faithful to it and will be forever fond of it. This analogy of my workmanship falls far short of what God is creating in me, but one thing I know—it is *my* book. And everyone else will know it is *my* book because it has *my* name on the cover. The book has been in my thoughts night and day. I keep forming and reforming it. There has been rewrite after rewrite. I have grown very fond of my book.

God is the Worker

The Almighty God is also creating masterpieces. He is forever fond of His workmanship, He is faithful to His work and, unlike me, He is never frustrated in His work. He is the potter, I am the clay. He is the artist, I am the canvas. He is the poet, I am the poem.

In Ephesians 2:10, Paul tells us, *"we are His workmanship created in Christ Jesus to good works."* We might wonder about thinking of God as a worker. But it is God who is at work with the work that He began when He chose to reach out in grace, to draw us unto His Son, to quicken us, and to regenerate us.

God's work is to take sinners, love them by His grace, and change them in a process whereby He will, one day, present them unto Himself glorious and without spot.

> *Christ also loved the church, and gave himself for it; that he might sanctify and cleanse it with the washing of water by the word, that he might present it to himself a glorious church, not having spot, or wrinkle, or any such thing; but that it should be holy and without blemish."* (Ephesians 5:25-27)

God is forever fond of His work. I know some of you don't like your jobs and might be wishing you could change jobs. But that's not the way it is with God. God likes His job and is forever fond of the work He is doing in us. The wonderful truth is that God is fond of us. The Bible says in Jeremiah (the Lord speaking) *"I have loved thee with an everlasting love"* (Jeremiah 31:3).

God is always faithful to His work. Some of us are not gifted or talented in doing odd jobs around the house. I hate to admit it, but I am one of them. Many times I give up and say, "I just can't do this!" But that's not the way it is with God. God is faithful to His work. *"He who began the good work in you will continue it"* (Philippians 1:6). His work in us will continue until the day Christ comes again. He won't give up on His workmanship.

God is never frustrated in His work. You and I are easily frustrated with our work. We may want to do something at our job, and our bosses won't let us. Maybe there are co-workers who don't contribute. We can't do our job the way we intend to do it, and we get frustrated. Not so with God!

I'm always a little leery of preachers who talk about God *trying* to do something. It rubs me the wrong way when people talk about God *attempting* to accomplish something, as though He might be unable to do it. How can that be? Is God like a man? Is He like us? Is He not able to do that which He determines to do?

WE ARE THE WORKMANSHIP

So we see that God is the worker, we are the workmanship. The word *workmanship* is the Greek word *poema,* from which we get our English word *poem*. In our English Bibles it is translated *workmanship,* but it literally means *masterpiece.* We, that is believers, the church, you and I, are His workmanship—His masterpieces.

God is at work in us, molding us into the image of His Son. We didn't even ask Him to do it. He chose to do it. As the potter molds the clay to be formed into the piece that He desires, so too God has us on His potter's wheel, forming us, making us, molding us into the very piece He desires us to be.

> ☙
> *God is forever fond of His work.*
> ☙

We are created. Do you think it is marvelous the way God created the universe? Frankly, even more marvelous is the way He has created you and me. We are created in Christ

Jesus. How remarkable it is to think about God taking us when we were spiritually dead and quickening us—making us alive by His grace. Then He is at work changing our character, changing our ways, changing our thought life, and changing our patterns—beginning on the day of grace, and continuing until the day of Christ.

We are crafted. God is continually crafting and forming us. A mysterious and majestic verse tells what God is doing: *"My little children, of whom I travail in birth* [that means of whom I am in pains of childbirth] *again until Christ be formed in you"* (Galatians 4:19 KJV). Paul is saying, "I am literally going through great pain as I watch God forming Christ in you. Sometimes I hurt when I see how He is molding and shaping you, because I know it hurts you. But just as a woman will go through the pains of childbirth because the blessing is wonderful, I, too, willingly go through childbirth pains because God is forming Christ in you."

GOD IS IN THE PROCESS OF FORMING AND CRAFTING US

His Spirit is placed in us. By His grace and eternal love for us as sinners, God has imparted His Spirit in us. When God began that work of grace in us, His Spirit took up residence in our hearts, and now lives within us and bears witness with our Spirits that we are children of God.

> *We become the tabernacle of the living God.*

God's Spirit began a work in us. He began to convict us of some things and to teach us some things. We suddenly found that heart of ours, which had been hard toward the things of God, began to soften. We found that somehow, some way, we were changing on the inside. We couldn't explain it.

People looked at us and said, "Wow, what's going on here?" Do you know what it was? God placed His Spirit in us, and we became the tabernacles of the living God.

Scriptures are proclaimed to us. Not only does God form us and craft us by giving us His Spirit, but we are also crafted by the Scriptures being proclaimed to us. The word of God is given to us and taken in, like a seed taking root in our hearts (I Peter 1:23). Then it blossoms into fruit.

When we hear the word proclaimed and taught to us, we take it in, and find that the word acts like a hammer to break down some hard walls around our hearts, or like a knife to cut where it needs to cut. But it is also like a balm, or medicine, that soothes where our hearts need to be soothed. The word can be an instrument and a tool of God as well as a comfort when applied to our hearts.

That's why, when we absent ourselves from the teaching of God's word, we feel as if we are spiritually sick because we are not being fed. The tools of God's word are not at work in our hearts because the Scriptures aren't being opened to us. But when we come to church and listen to the teaching of God's word, we find ourselves growing in our walk with Christ. We find ourselves convicted of sin. We find ourselves learning things and reveling in the love of God.

Situations are put around us. God forms and crafts us by the situations that are placed around us. Our earthly fathers discipline us because they love us. So how much more does our Heavenly Father love us enough to discipline us?

When we go to the gymnasium, our trainers put us through exercises to strengthen us. That's what our Heavenly Father does. He places us in circumstances to form Christ within us. As a result, we can rejoice even in our sufferings because God is at work forming our character.

I have a gentle word of caution for anyone who is praying that God would remove difficult circumstances from his or her life. Even though this might be His will for us; recognize that sometimes these situations are placed around us in order that Christ be formed in us.

WE ARE CREATED FOR GOOD WORKS

He created us, He is crafting us, and He changes us. How are we changed? We are changed from a *no*-gooder to a *do*-gooder.

In Ephesians 2:10 we find that *"we are His workmanship, created in Christ Jesus unto good works,"* but Romans 3:12 says, *"There is none that does good, no not one."*

If *"none do good"* how can we be created unto good works? It is only possible because it is God who is at work. It is God who is making us into what He wants us to be in order that we might do good. You say, "Well, He has a lot of work to do in me!" I know He does. He has a lot of work to do in all of us.

I want to give some encouragement. Some of you are struggling spiritually. You're fighting. You're trying to do good in order to earn the favor of God. You're trying to do good works in order for God to bless you. Some of you think you should be going to the mission field or full time ministry, and you feel guilty because you're not there. You're striving to do good. Relax!

When God graced us, He put us on that potter's wheel by which He molds us; He put us on His canvas by which He makes us His masterpiece. He is working to make us into the very thing He wants us to be! So just rest in Him and watch Him,

---
God is the worker, we are the workmanship.
---

through His Spirit, change you from the inside out. Watch Him, through His word, do a work in you week after week. Watch Him as He forms you and crafts you through His Spirit, through His word, and through your situations. Just rest in His work.

Remember, God is the worker, we are the workmanship. Don't get it reversed. You are not the worker.

The Evidence of His Workmanship

Good works are an indication that God has graced us. *"Faith without works is dead"* (James 2:17). Anyone who says, "I have faith in Christ, my sins are forgiven," but does not have good works is spiritually dead. He is a liar. He is not alive in Christ but remains dead, for faith without works is dead.

Our salvation, as well as our good works, are gifts of grace. *"For by grace are you saved through faith; and that not of yourselves: it is the gift of God: not of works, lest any man should boast"* (Ephesians 2:8, 9). Paul tells us that even our good works are gifts of grace and, in fact, are *evidence* of saving faith. *"For we are His workmanship, created in Christ Jesus unto good works, which God hath before ordained that we should walk in them"* (Ephesians 2:10).

The reason I believe in the eternal security of the believer ("once saved, always saved") is because my salvation is the work of God—not the work of myself. And the reason I am not struggling and striving with the concept of good works is that even my good works are the work of God. So why should I worry, and why should I boast? *God* is the worker, I am *His* workmanship.

A desire to follow Christ is evidence that He has begun the work. Even though our walk may be far from perfect, others should be able to tell that we have a desire to follow after Him.

If you have no desire to follow Christ, if the things of God mean nothing to you, then you are not His workmanship yet. I'll pray for you that He will put you on His canvas. I'll pray that He will begin that work. I'll pray that you will come to know the God who saves sinners.

All we have to do if we want Him to begin the work is just call to Him. He never turns away a cry for mercy. Call to Him right now, right where you are! He'll begin the work.

God has designed our lives so that *He* may be glorified. We don't do good in order to impress others and impress God. If we boast to others about our works, that is evidence that *we* would be glorified. *He* has designed our lives, *He* has ordained us unto good works, so that *He* may be glorified. Whoever you are—whether you're a schoolteacher, a painter, a preacher—whatever you're doing; you are *His* workmanship. Rest in it.

Not everyone will understand what you're going through. Some who witness what is going on will not like the changes. When God changes you, some will laugh. When God touches you by His grace, that heart of yours that used to love sin will change and will begin to hate sin; and some won't understand.

That husband who hates the thought of your going to church because you are finding contentment and peace apart from him won't understand. He won't understand your relationship with Christ. But it's all right, because you have a relationship with the One who has formed you, is fond of you, and will never give up on you. The security you have in your relationship with Him will encourage you to show compassion, even for those who are not comfortable with the changes they are seeing in you.

WE ARE CHANGED FROM THE INSIDE OUT

God is not passive. He is not just sitting back, watching, and thinking, "Now what are *you* going to do for *Me*?" No—God is active, changing us, molding us, forming us, and shaping us into the image of His Son. His work, which is so amazing, makes us followers of Christ from the inside out.

> *God is crafting us into the image of His Son.*

No longer do we need rules, laws, and regulations to obey God. They are on the inside, written and planted in our hearts. *"After these days, says the Lord, I will put my law in their inward parts, and write it in their hearts"* (Jeremiah 31:33b). We follow Him just because that's the way we are. We know when we fail Him (like we all do). Our hearts are such that we know we have sinned, and we repent of it because we have a new nature. The dog returns to its vomit, but we don't. When we go back to those old patterns of living, it hurts because the Spirit lives within us. So we just go to the Lord Jesus and confess to Him.

We begin to see that God is not so much interested in what we do as in who we are. He is forming us into the very persons He wants us to be.

If we've been touched by Christ and come to Him in saving faith—trusting and reclining upon Him for all of our needs—that is evidence God has begun a work in us, and *we are* His workmanship. God is fond of His work, which *we are*; He is faithful to His work, which *we are*; and He will never give up on His work, which *we are*. He is molding and crafting us into what He wants us to be in order that we might do good. He is forming Christ in us for the purpose of presenting us unto Himself—glorious and without spot. It is a process, so it might take some time, but He has begun the work in all who know Him.

A lady in my church once said to me, "Pastor, I grew up in a tradition where I was taught that you do the best you can for God, that you believe that Christ died for your sins, and then you just really worked hard. If you were away from God and not working for Him and doing good, you lost His favor and His love. So what you've got to do is recommit yourself and tell God you're going to try harder to do the best you can. I am so tired from working so hard trying to please God that I feel like a fallen sparrow with its feet pointed to the sky—too weak and tired to have the energy to fly."

My friend, stop being a spiritual sparrow! It is the Almighty God who is at work in you. He's fond of His work, faithful to it, and never frustrated with it. He's creating you into a new person, changing you day by day, and crafting you into the image of His Son.

In his book, *Mere Christianity*, C. S. Lewis shares an illustration that came from George MacDonald:

> Imagine yourself as a living house. God comes in to rebuild that house. At first, perhaps, you can understand what He is doing. He is getting the drains right and stopping the leaks in the roof and so on: you knew that those jobs needed doing and so you are not surprised. But presently He starts knocking the house about in a way that hurts abominably and does not seem to make sense. What on earth is He up to? The explanation is that He is building quite a different house from the one you thought of—throwing out a new wing here, putting on an extra floor there, running up towers, making courtyards. You thought you were going to be made into a decent little cottage: but He is building a palace. He intends to come and live in it Himself.[1]

When all the chosen Ones
shall be gathered together,
and the church of God in heaven
shall be perfect, not one living stone
lacking of the entire fabric,
then across that edifice shall this
inscription be written in letters of light,
"To the praise of the glory of his grace."

C. H. Spurgeon

Dei Gratia

FOR THE PRAISE
OF HIS GRACE

To the praise of the glory of his grace.
Ephesians 1:6

When we come to the place of realizing that God is under no obligation to give grace, and that He does not favor every sinner with forgiveness, adoption, justification, and every other gift of grace given to His people; the inevitable question that arises is "Why?"

Why me?

Why has God given His Son for us? Why has God opened our eyes to believe in His Son? Why has God delivered us from the awful condemnation of sin? Why has God graciously given us purpose and guidance in this life?

Paul gives us the answer in Ephesians 1:6, *"For the praise of His grace."*

A SONG OF DELIVERANCE

After the Israelites had been delivered from captivity (which is an Old Testament picture of the church being delivered from the bondage of sin by God's grace), Miriam, the sister of Moses, took a timbrel in her hand, and all the women took timbrels in their hands and went out with singing and dancing. They sang, *"Sing ye to the Lord, for he hath triumphed gloriously; the horse and his rider hath he thrown into the sea"* (Exodus 15:21).

In Deuteronomy 32:1-43, Moses sings of Israel's deliverance with thanksgiving and praise. Several of the Psalms are hymns of praise recounting Israel's history. Even the saints in heaven will sing the song of Moses, as well as the song of the Lamb (Revelation 15:3).

Like the children of Israel, we too can sing the wonderful song of redemption for the Lord *has* triumphed gloriously with each of us. The horse and rider of our sin, rebellion, and captivity He *has* thrown into the sea.

In 1870, C. H. Spurgeon delivered a message on the "praise of the glory of God's grace." This powerful sermon was called *"Dei Gratia."* In it Spurgeon said that he wished for a "tongue more fluent" than his to praise the glory of God's grace. But then he said what is wanted is "no tongue but a warm heart and grateful thought to sit down and contemplate."

I wish I could insert here a section of silence. I would ask you today (as Spurgeon asked his congregation over a century ago), "now in silence to praise God while your mind surveys the whole plan of your salvation." I would ask you to contemplate, and remember, and rehearse, and repeat your redemption.

Your Personal Deliverance

Look back over the "I am ——" chapters of this book, and reflect on what each of these statements means to you. Remember how God has saved you, by His **grace**, in spite of your positive *de*-merit. Remember how God has **loved** you unconditionally. Remember how God has **justified** you by dealing with the guilt of your sin on the cross. Remember how God has **chosen** you and will never *un*choose you. Remember how God *has* **blessed** you with *all* spiritual blessings. Remember how God has set you **free** from bondage to sin, Satan, and the law. Remember how God has **protected** you, so you no longer need live in fear. Remember that you are **adopted** and have the privilege of calling God, *abba*, Father. Remember that you are **guided** even though you might not be able to see the way. Remember that you are 100% **holy** because you are clothed in the holiness of Christ. Remember that you are **accepted** by God and, therefore, can accept others. Remember that you are **rewarded** as a joint heir with the Son. Remember that you are **His** workmanship.

Remember all of this, and write your song of redemption. Write your song of deliverance, and then sing that song over and over and over and over.

Hallelujah!

If you have trouble writing your song, just go to the Psalms. In Hebrew, the Psalms are called the *halim,* which in English means "*the praises*." This is where we get the word *hallelujah. Hallelujah* is Hebrew for *praise the Lord.*

How Do We Praise God?

How do we praise our own children? How do we bless them?

Let's say your daughter is playing basketball, and she makes a rebound or a good pass. What do you do? You shout out your praise. If it were possible, you would praise your child by running out on the court, getting hold of her, and whispering your words of praise in her ear.

When was the last time you got hold of God? When was the last time you came into His presence? When was the last time you lifted up your hands and worshipped Him? You say, "Physically or spiritually?" Either, it makes no difference.

When the Old Testament Jew worshipped God, he would worship with his hands uplifted. Some of the earliest paintings of Christians (which are found in the catacombs of Rome) show them with uplifted hands. The uplifted hand is not only a token of receiving blessings from God, but also an expression of apprehending the Lord who has bestowed blessings. Is it any wonder that in the Hebrew language there are twelve words for worship which use the word *hand*?

We Baptists are timid about lifting our hands. We ought not be so. Worship of God, praise of Him, is an overflow of our understanding of what He has done for us. When was the last time you worshipped Him from the overflow of your heart?

Praise to God Is Not Prayer to God

Some people think when they pray they are worshipping God—but not necessarily. Prayer is a good thing, but praise is a different matter. Prayer is not praise. The old Puritan,

Thomas Matten, said: "Self love leads us to prayer. But love to God excites us to praise."

We will only get hold of God in real praise when we comprehend grace. We can only "praise the glory of his grace" when we understand that grace.

That is why I have written this book on learning contentment by knowing who we are, as well as what we have, with God's grace. My purpose has been to show the grace that God has given you and me and to set before you the gifts of God.

Hopefully, you have received the good news, taken it in, and now your heart can surge with praise. I hope this book has taught you to receive your circumstances as a gift from God and praise Him for them. I hope you have found out exactly what God thinks of you and what He, by His grace, has done for you.

> 80
> *Self love leads us to prayer.*
> *But love to God*
> *excites us to praise.*
> 80

I want to fill you with the assurance that you can freely worship the Lord because you can come into God's presence without blame. I want your heart to overflow with praise because you know what God has done for you.

UNSTIFLE THE PRAISE

Maybe you are not overflowing with praise. You may have read other books that tell you the "victorious" Christian will have a life with no problems. You might not be overflowing in praise or feel you are growing in grace because you see sin, suffering, and pain in your life.

Do you have sin in your life? Praise God that you have recognized it is sin. Praise God that He has paid the penalty for that sin on the cross. Praise God that you can bring that sin to Him, and the Holy Spirit can work within you to free you from besetting sins and harmful habits.

According to Spurgeon, in *Dei Gratia*, God is more glorified in the redemption of sinners through Jesus and His grace than if one had never sinned. But Spurgeon goes on to say that we must not think we have to be great sinners so God will be more glorified. He says you may have heard powerful testimonies of vile sinners who have become a trophy of God's grace. It makes you feel as if you have no testimony because you have not committed any dramatic sins that show the power of God to transform a life. But Spurgeon warns: "Do not for a moment . . . put sin in the place of merit . . . If there be no reason for grace in human merit, much less in the degree of demerit."

If you are the worst of sinners—praise God. If you are the least of sinners—praise God.

Are you suffering? You may not be overflowing with praise because you are in the middle of suffering and pain. Maybe you have a serious illness or have lost a loved one. It may be that your children are in trouble or your marriage is failing.

All you can ask is, "Why? Why? Why? Why is God allowing this to happen to me?"

See suffering for what it is. Suffering is finite—God's blessings are infinite. We will all suffer at various times and in various degrees until the day we stand before God, face to face, and His work in us is complete.

In Chapter Fourteen of this book, we see that suffering is the threshold into the very presence of God Himself. *"We*

suffer with Him, that we may be also glorified together"
(Romans 8:17). Receive your suffering as a gift from God.
Your present suffering is not worthy to be compared to
"the glory revealed in us" (Romans 8:18).

If you are suffering—praise God. If you are not suffering—praise God.

Why didn't God just make the world a better place to
begin with? Why did He allow sin, suffering, and pain to be
part of His creation? Wouldn't He be more glorified with a
more perfect world?

We live in a defiled world that has been cursed because of
Adam's sin, but one day the origi-
nal harmony and order of the
universe will be restored. So why
did God curse creation if He was
going to restore it? He did it for
the "praise of the glory of His grace." Spurgeon says that
God is more glorified in the transformation of decay than the
maintaining of the original purity.

> *If you are suffering—praise God. If you are not suffering—praise God.*

Are you successful? The key to contentment is learning
to praise God even when we are not experiencing prosperity,
comfort, and success. Robert Haldane says, "If you promise
to yourself in this life perpetual enjoyment of ease and
prosperity, you miscalculate the times, and confuse the
present with the future."

I watch football games where some of the men on the
winning team are believers. They love the Lord and are not
ashamed to share their faith in Christ. When I see some of
them being interviewed after the game, they give glory to
Christ for the victory. That's good. I would never condemn
anyone for doing that.

But sometimes I cringe because I feel many make the mistake of thinking that we can only praise God when we're a success—when we win. I wish someone would be interviewed who had just lost a game and hear them say, "I want to give glory to Jesus Christ."

If you are successful—praise God; if you are unsuccessful —praise God.

"Blessed Be the God and Father of Our Lord Jesus Christ"

Paul, the writer of Ephesians, was a prisoner. He was not "winning" in the world's eyes. He was not a success in the world's eyes—he was a poor man. But he began his letter to the Ephesians by praising the Lord:

> *Blessed be the God and Father of our Lord Jesus Christ, who hath blessed us with all spiritual blessings in heavenly places in Christ; According as He hath chosen us in Him before the foundation of the world, that we should be holy and without blame before Him in love; Having predestinated us unto the adoption of children by Jesus Christ to himself, according to the good pleasure of his will. To the praise of the glory of his grace, wherein he hath made us accepted in the beloved.*
> (Ephesians 1:3-6 KJV)

Look at the first word, *blessed*. "*Blessed be the God and Father of our Lord Jesus Christ.*" That word *blessed* is sometimes translated *praise*. In Greek it is *eulogetos*, the word from which we get our English word *eulogy*. The literal translation is *good word*. Paul the poor, unsuccessful prisoner, is offering a eulogy of praise unto the Lord!

WHAT CAN WE PRAISE HIM FOR?

Anyone can bless God for temporal blessings. Anyone can praise God for good things that happen in this life. Only a believer can learn how to bless God for *spiritual* blessings.

We can praise Him for the glory of His grace in our salvation. God arranged our salvation. The Son accomplished our salvation. He lived a sinless life in our place. This innocent Man died a sinful death in the place of guilty sinners like us. All of our sins were placed upon Him. God separates them from us as far as the east is from the west.

Our destiny is eternal, and our destiny is sure because God has done the saving. A. W. Pink says there is no "hope" in the salvation of the soul. The believer is not "trying to live up to the light that he has," he is not "doing his best," and hoping that somehow everything will come out right in the end. Our salvation

> 𝕰
> *There is no "hope"*
> *in the salvation*
> *of the soul.*
> 𝕰

is not some vague and uncertain hope that we will go to heaven at the last. Our salvation is present-tense, simple, and definite. We already possess it.

Spurgeon says we don't just praise God for the entire grand plan of salvation from first to last as a whole, but also for each detail of salvation. When we, by the wonderful grace of God, find ourselves to be in Christ, His righteousness is ours. "We do not have to obey God's commandments, walk worthy, and serve the Lord, in order to become God's children, we are to do these things because we are, already, members of the household of faith."

We can praise Him for our perserverance of faith in Christ. When we came to faith in Jesus Christ, we were going our own way, doing our own thing. But the Spirit graciously arrested us and began to do a work in us that He will finish. He will not give up until the day of Christ, until we see the Lord Jesus.

When we begin to see that He started that good work and will carry it on, we will begin to understand that we are secure in the grace of God. God has our name written on the palm of His hand. He has captured us. The grip of grace is an irrevocable grip—a grip of power. He sustains us by the right hand of His Almighty power.

The Almighty God accomplished the work of salvation and provided the gifts of grace for His people for one reason—"*for the praise of the glory of His grace.*"

I Am Confused

The teachings in this book may be so far removed from what you have believed and been taught that you are completely confused. It is more than your mind can handle. You are shocked by grace.

I want to encourage you not to *confuse yourself* with the issues of God's eternal grace. No—*strengthen yourself* with what you have read here, and share it with someone you love.

This book is good news for broken sinners. If a broken sinner recognizes that he or she can't do anything to receive God's grace but turn to Christ, who saves sinners, it should encourage his or her heart.

So take this good news, *share it with others,* and watch what God does. That loved one you're concerned for—that mother, that father, that husband, that wife, that child—who doesn't know Christ, get on your knees and pray for that one. Then share the glorious truth of God's grace.

HIS STORY—YOUR STORY

Spurgeon speaks of:

> "certain skeptical philosophers" who have half conceded that there may have been an exhibition of divine strength in the beginning, when the great orbs of heaven were first caused to revolve, but then they affect to question whether any fresh power is put forth to preserve the stars in their courses; but you and I know that . . . the Divine Power is always streaming forth to urge on the wheels of the universe.
>
> It is even so in the little world within us.

In the past few years my wife, Rachelle, says she has been having a growing sense that all things, not only in her life but also in the universe, are working out according to the purpose of God. Knowing this has given her a great sense of peace. This, my friend, is praise of His grace.

John Piper says:

> If you are trusting in Jesus Christ ... the roots of your life were planted in the eternal counsels of God, and the branches of your life are growing into an absolutely sure and glorious future with God. There are no unimportant days in your life. You don't ever have to go to bed at night feeling that your life is going nowhere. You don't ever have to give in to the lie that you are not connected to an awesome purpose.[1]

All of *history* is *His story*. All of *your story* is *His story*.

Take time now to reflect upon your story. Then recite it, rehearse it, remember it, and repeat it. Sing your story over and over and over again for *"the praise of the glory of His grace."*

A Discussion Guide

INTRODUCTION

1. Why does it seem impossible to be happy regardless of our circumstances?

2. Which is easier for you: to *do* something for God or *learn* something from God?

3. Look at the titles of Chapters 3-15 in the Table of Contents. Which of these means the most to you? Which are the most difficult to accept?

4. How does God teach His children things they need to know?

5. How would your life be different if there were a deep, abiding joy regardless of your circumstances?

Chapter 1 - UNHAPPINESS HAPPENS

1. Are you unhappy? Why? What do you believe needs to change in order to make you happy?

2. What things have you tried in your "pursuit of happiness"? How would you describe the happiness you received from them?

3. Do you see any of the five marks of discontentment in your life?

4. Do any of these marks of discontentment that you might experience signify a deficient understanding of God's grace to you?

5. Have you known anyone who seemed happy but was not? Why were you surprised when you discovered he or she was not really happy?

Chapter 2 - THE KEY TO HAPPINESS

1. Are you uncomfortable with desiring to be happy? If so, why?

2. Read Philippians 4. What is the background of Paul's situation? What is your situation? Can you learn from Paul?

3. In what ways are you looking to others or circumstances for your happiness? List them.

4. Is it easy for you to see the extent of your own unhappiness or is it easier to see unhappiness in others?

5. Describe the "key to genuine happiness" in your own words.

Chapter 3 - I AM GRACED

1. How does God grace the undeserving? How has God graced you?

2. What do you deserve from God?

3. List some of the things you have been led to believe you must do in order to receive God's favor or grace.

4. Read Romans 8:32. Is grace limited to your salvation only? If not, what else?

5. What are some things in your life that you think might make you undeserving of God's favor?

Chapter 4 - I Am Loved

1. When have you received *conditional* love, from a human perspective? When have you received *unconditional* love, from a human perspective?

2. List some things you are doing in order to try to please God. Do you think He will love you more if you do these things?

3. Why does God love you?

4. Read Psalm 139. Do you, like David, find yourself hiding from God? Why?

5. Does God love everyone with an unconditional love? Explain.

6. What is your response to His unconditional love for you?

Chapter 5 - I Am Justified

1. Are you guilty before God? Why or why not?

2. Does it seem we freely talk about pardon (forgiveness) and rarely about justification? Why?

3. What things have you done in order to try to be justified in God's eyes?

4. Which is more important: faith in Christ or the work of Christ?

5. Why don't people see a need to be justified by God?

Chapter 6 - I Am Chosen

1. Does the idea of being "chosen" scare you? What have you been taught about election?

2. Who has been chosen? Read I Corinthians 1:26-31. Does being chosen by God lead to pride or humility? Why?

3. Why do people get angry with the idea that God chooses?

4. How do you know if *you* are chosen by God?

5. What things do you choose in life and why do you choose them? How is this different from God's choice to save sinners?

Chapter 7 - I Am Blessed

1. Read Ephesians 1:3. When *do* you receive blessings from God? What must you do to be *fully* blessed?

2. Where do we get our misconceptions about blessing?

3. Many verses are quoted to us promising God's blessing if we do certain things (pray, repent). Where do most of these verses come from? What is the difference between the Old Covenant and the New Covenant?

4. How does our understanding of blessings affect our relationship with others?

5. Why do you do what you do for God? Finish the sentence: "I believe God will bless me more if I ——."

Chapter 8 - I Am Free

1. "The Christian life should be measured by freedom." True or False? Explain.

2. Are you afraid of freedom? List some things that keep you from being free.

3. Why can we say that "God sees no sin in His people"?

4. Respond to this statement: "The church, the Christian, and the gospel, are not so much concerned about removing the occasions for sin, as in removing from man the desire to sin."

5. How does true freedom remove the desire to sin?

Chapter 9 - I Am Protected

1. What is godly fear? What is ungodly fear?

2. Read II Timothy 1:7. Where does fear come from?

3. What are five fears of those without grace? Which of those fears are you experiencing? Why are you experiencing fear in these areas?

4. What can we do when we are experiencing fear?

5. Explain how God can work all things—even bad things—for our good.

Chapter 10 - I Am Adopted

1. Who has the right to call God, "Father"?

2. What are some of the special privileges of calling God, "Father"?

3. What is the difference between a child and a slave?

4. When will we truly understand our adoption?

5. Why should an adopted child know he or she is truly loved?

Chapter 11 - I Am Guided

1. How does being guided affect how you live day-to-day?

2. If you don't want to believe you are guided, then who do you believe is in control of your life?

3. What are the characteristics of the providence of God?

4. How do you make difficult choices? If you sense you are guided, then how can you make difficult choices?

5. Read James 4:15 and I Samuel 3:18. What are the limitations of the plans you make?

6. In which areas of your life do you most sense God's guidance? Are there areas of your life that you feel are apart from the guidance of God?

Chapter 12 - I Am Holy

1. How holy would you say that you are?

2. List some ways you are trying to be holy. If you could do all of these perfectly, would it make you more holy?

3. How is being holy an "impossible possiblity"?

4. Why is it hard for people to accept that "Jesus is our holiness"?

5. Do you generally find it more difficult to *receive* something or to *give* something? Why? How does this apply to holiness and your relationship with God?

Chapter 13 - I Am Accepted

1. What can cause God to reject you?

2. List some ways you have felt rejection from others.

3. How has rejection affected your relationships with God and others?

4. What is the root of feelings of rejection?

5. Why is it so important to trust in God's unconditional acceptance of you? What will it do for the body of Christ?

Chapter 14 - I Am Rewarded

1. What rewards are you expecting? Why?

2. Why is the subject of rewards debatable? What are some of the wrong directions we can go in our understanding of rewards? What problems can be caused by a false teaching of rewards?

3. Is God fair? Is God just? Is God right? Read Matthew 20:1-16.

4. Where does suffering come from? Is it a curse or a reward?

5. Do you believe Christians will face any judgment by God? Why?

Chapter 15 – I Am His

1. Read Ephesians 2:10. Are you God's masterpiece? How has God created His masterpiece in you? How is He crafting and forming you?

2. How does God regard His workmanship? How does God regard you?

3. Is God's work finished in you?

4. What are some things you are doing to try to improve God's workmanship in your life?

5. Does God ever fail in any work He begins? Give biblical illustrations if possible.

For the Praise of His Glory

1. Read Ephesians 1:6. Why did God give His Son for you and all the gifts associated with His grace?

2. Take time to write your personal story of the grace of God in your life.

3. Look at the titles of Chapters 3–15 in the Table of Contents. Can you say "I am ——" to each of these?

4. Prayer to God is not praise to God. True or false? Discuss.

5. What keeps you from praising God?

6. As you have read this book, what has confused you the most? Are you "shocked by grace"? If so, then be strengthened with what you have learned and find someone with whom to share the good news of his or her identity in Christ.

NOTES

Chapter 1 – UNHAPPINESS HAPPENS
[1]Paul Burleson, my father, has a ministry to pastors and staff members. He conducts one-day conferences and men's retreats. He pastored churches in Texas and Oklahoma for over forty years.
[2]Max Lucado, *A Love Worth Giving*, (Nashville: W Publishing Group, 2002), 36-38.

Chapter 2 – THE KEY TO HAPPINESS
[1]Philip Yancy, *Soul Survivor*, (New York: Doubleday, 2001), 57-58.
[2]My appreciation to John Daily, Oklahoma Coordinator of Point Man Ministries, an organization which provides support for veterans and their families. <http://www.pointmanok.com>

Chapter 3 – I AM GRACED
[1]C. S. Lewis, *Mere Christianity*, (New York: Macmillan Publishing Company, 1952), 39.
[2]C. S. Lewis, *Surprised by Joy*, (San Diego: Harcourt Brace & Company, 1956), 228.
[3]Rod Rosenblat quoted in Michael Horton, *Putting Amazing Back into Grace* (Grand Rapids: Baker, 1991), 158-159.
[4]Charles Swindoll, *The Grace Awakening*, (Dallas: Word, 1990), 44.

Chapter 4 – I AM LOVED
[1]John Blanchard, *Gathered Gold*, comp. John Blanchard (Hertfordshire: Evangelical Press, 1984), 118.
Unless otherwise noted, most of the quotations in *Happiness Doesn't Just Happen* are from this invaluable resource.
[2]A. W. Tozer, *The Knowledge of the Holy*, (San Francisco: HarperSanFrancisco, 1961), 153.

Chapter 6 – I AM CHOSEN
[1]John Blanchard, *Gathered Gold,* 73.

Chapter 8 – I Am Free
[1]Steve Brown, *When Being Good Isn't Good Enough,* (Grand Rapids, Michigan: Baker Books, 1990), 155-167.

Chapter 11 – I Am Guided
[1]C. S. Lewis, "The Efficacy of Prayer," *Fern-seed and Elephants* (Glasgow: Collins, 1982), 96.
[2]J. R. R. Tolkien, *The Lord of the Rings,* (New York: Houghton Mifflin Company, 1994), 264.
[3]J. R. R. Tolkien, *The Lord of the Rings,* 60-61.

Chapter 12 – I Am Holy
[1]Peter Lord, *Turkeys and Eagles,* (Auburn, Maine: The SeedSowers, 1987), 99.

Chapter 14 – I Am Rewarded
[1]John Piper, "Blessed Are the Persecuted," March 16, 1986, <http://www.desiringgod.org/library/sermons/86/031686.html>
[2]C. S. Lewis, "The Weight of Glory," *The Weight of Glory and Other Addresses,* (Grand Rapids, Michigan: William B. Eerdmans Publishing Company, 1979), 10.
[3]C. S. Lewis, "The Weight of Glory," 7.
[4]Don Fortner, "Will There be Degrees of Reward in Heaven?" <http://www.sovereign-grace.com/doctrine/gcdoc0071.htm>
[5]C. S. Lewis, "The Weight of Glory," 9, 10.

Chapter 15 – I Am His
[1] C. S. Lewis, *Mere Christianity*, (New York: Macmillan Publishing Company, 1952), 174.

For the Praise of His Grace
[1]John Piper, "God's Invincible Purposes," <http://www.soundofgrace.com/piper92/03-08-92.htm>

Give the gift of:

Happiness
DOESN'T JUST
HAPPEN

ORDER FORM

Yes, I want____copies of *HAPPINESS DOESN'T JUST HAPPEN*
for $12.95 each. Include $3 shipping and handling.
Oklahoma residents include $1.08 (8.35%) sales tax.
Payment must accompany orders. Allow 3 weeks for delivery.

My check or money order for $_____is enclosed.

Please charge my ☐Visa ☐MasterCard

Card#_____

Exp. Date_____Signature_____

Name_____

Address_____

City/State/Zip_____

Phone_____e-mail_____

Phone 580 237 0602
Fax 580 237 0662
Make your check payable and return to:
York Street Press
2505 West Garriott   Enid, OK 73703
http://www.emmanuel-baptist.org